Youth Work from Scratch

By the same author and published by Monarch Books
The Ideas Factory
The Think Tank
The Beautiful Disciplines
500 Prayers for Young People

Youth Work from Scratch

How to launch or revitalize a church youth project

Martin Saunders

MONARCH
BOOKS

Oxford, UK & Grand Rapids, Michigan, USA

Published by Monarch Books
an imprint of
Lion Hudson plc
Wilkinson House, Jordan Hill Road,
Oxford OX2 8DR, England
Email: monarch@lionhudson.com
www.lionhudson.com/monarch

ISBN 978 0 85721 256 6
e-ISBN 978 0 85721 464 5

First edition 2013

Acknowledgments
Scripture quotations are taken from the Holy Bible, New International Version Anglicised. Copyright © 1979, 1984, 2011 Biblica, formerly International Bible Society. Used by permission of Hodder & Stoughton Ltd, an Hachette UK company. All rights reserved. "NIV" is a registered trademark of Biblica. UK trademark number 1448790. Scripture quotations marked "NLT" are taken from the *Holy Bible* New Living Translation. Copyright © 1996, 2004. Used by permission of Tyndale House Publishers, Inc., Carol Stream, Illinois 60188. All rights reserved

A catalogue record for this book is available from the British Library

Printed and bound in the UK, April 2013, LH27

To the teams behind *Youthwork* magazine and the
Youthwork Summit.
Your passion for God and for young people makes
me never want to leave youth ministry.

Contents

Foreword

Gavin Calver

As is so often the case on a Sunday morning, the alarm rang early and I dragged myself out of my cosy bed to take to the motorway and drive for miles to speak at a church. Don't get me wrong, I always enjoy it, but leaving home first thing is a challenge! Today I had the privilege of talking to a congregation of a couple of hundred, mainly dominated by young families and the more mature. It was a great time of witnessing God at work amongst His people. However, it always stirs me up to see less than a handful of young people present – and challenges me to think about what kind of "church" we are encouraging them to join. Apparently on this particular morning they had stayed in the service because the preacher was deemed "accessible" for them! After the service had ended and I had chatted to members of the church, the vicar asked me to meet him in his study for a coffee. Before I could even sit down he chucked a question at me that I have been asked hundreds, if not thousands, of times, "How can we get more young people in our church?"

In the twelve years I have worked for Youth for Christ this question has been asked more than any other. Whether it is asked by church leaders or members of the congregation, they see a problem and this is the question they think will generate all the right answers. As if there is some sort of pithy solution to the massive issue of the missing generations in our churches! Equally I often want to ask a different question back: "Do you actually want young people or do you want young-looking old people?" Do we really want churches full of teenagers, or is it more about our church photograph looking complete by covering the full age spectrum?

Into this reality I so welcome this wonderful book from my friend Martin Saunders. In essence it helps those churches who want to reach young people for Christ; to assist them in starting a youth ministry in as simple a way as possible. He begins with a powerful and persuasive look at why we should work with teenagers. I need no convincing but nonetheless found his argument clear and compelling. In truth, as I travel the nation it becomes clearer all the time that the church wants to get behind youth ministry. It is keen to reach new generations and is prepared to pray, invest, and consider the change required. It is a clear "Yes, but how?" moment. Yes, we want to have thriving youth ministry, but how on earth might this even begin to be achieved?

Martin absolutely excels in answering this "how?" question. This book is greatly inspiring, but moreover it is profoundly practical. There is no great need for a youth ministry book that aims to win over hearts and minds – what we need is a pragmatic "how to". His use of very practical steps and linear approaches to things is so simple and if followed faithfully will prove greatly effective. I also think that the constant signposting to other youth ministries and help is excellent, as is the input from numerous youth specialists, making the content even more valuable. The FAQ section is not to be missed and I think will provide a regular return point for many. Martin is a genius at making the most of all his own knowledge as well as being hugely resourceful in collating that of his large address book.

I agree with Martin's suggestion that someone newer to youth ministry should read the book right through and follow what it suggests. Don't underestimate the quality of the forms and links included too. They may seem simple but are certainly effective and worth using fully. However as someone who has been in youth ministry for over a decade I also found it hugely helpful reading. Yes, a lot of it was refreshment, but it would not hurt any youth worker to read the lot. In fact I would go as far as to say that anyone in youth ministry would not regret reading every word in this book and should get hold of a copy right away.

Buy this book, turn every page, and then get involved. We need as many people as possible getting active in youth ministry as soon as they can. I know that so many believe that the outlook is bleak for the church, but personally I believe that the future of the church in this nation is better than its past. Yet this cannot just be words – we must act, and that is why I am so grateful for this brilliant book. It gives a solution to a definite problem in an accessible and easy way.

I will have a box of these in my car. That way every time someone else asks me "how can we get more young people in our church?" I will at least have a resource to hand them and help them begin to answer that fundamental question.

Gavin Calver, National Director, Youth for Christ, Halesowen

Introduction

You are an incredibly important and brilliant human being. Why? Because you care enough about young people to have picked up this book and started reading. You are concerned enough about a generation who have been stigmatized by the media, who have seen their dreams crushed by a failing economic system; you believe that same generation are still capable not only of forging their own bright future but also of shaping ours. You see their potential. You love their passion. You, my friend, are someone special: you're a youth worker.

Now, don't get hung up on those two words. You might not be employed to mentor teenagers in a local café; you may not even be on a rota to drive the youth-club minibus. You could be pretty much anyone – but if you're reading this book because you want, in some small way, to make a difference to the lives of young people, then for the purposes of these pages you're a youth worker. The church needs more people to recognize that they can make a contribution to its ministry among young people. In fact, we need a church *full* of youth workers.

That said, you are most likely to be in one of two broad groups. Either you are taking this book at its word and are looking to set up a youth-work initiative for the first time, or you are seeking to breathe new life into a project that seems to have lost momentum. If the former, I'd humbly suggest you might want to read this resource in a linear fashion; if the latter, you may want to adopt a more pick 'n' mix approach to the content. If at any time you find me boring, whatever your context, do feel free to silence my self-important droning by skipping ahead.

If either of these broad categories does describe your situation, then once again I salute you. You have recognized not only that young people are well worth your time and energy, but also that, without them, the church of today simply doesn't have a tomorrow. I hope this book – which has been crafted by a small army of passionate youth workers just like you – will be a real help as you try to build a better future both for young people and for your church – and a better present too.

Why?

You've decided to get involved in youth ministry. Why?

It's a pretty good and important first question. And, at one level, I can't possibly know the answer or hope to provide one. Working with young people is alternately the most rewarding and the most demanding ministry I know of: no one gets into it for the money, the fame, or the glory. On a personal level, either you have had a sense of calling (or vocation) or a persuasive phone call from a church or local leader, or you've realized that no one else is rolling their sleeves up to serve young people in your community. So I'm not really asking why you've picked up this book; rather I'm asking – why should any of us bother with youth ministry?

A gospel for everyone

Most simply, the answer to that is that God clearly doesn't have a lower age limit in mind when he invites us into relationship with him. Jesus staggered the disciples with his request to "let the little children come to me" (Matthew 19:14), because, in their culture, children were lesser citizens, intended to be seen and not heard. It seemed preposterous to them that a rabbi would be interested in children who were not yet of an age at which they might traditionally begin their discipleship. Yet Jesus is – and He goes further, pointing out that childlike faith is something not just to be cherished, but to be aimed for in adulthood. Obviously Jesus isn't advocating childish and immature theology, but the idea of a *childlike* approach to faith is very positive: one which accepts a higher authority; which has no place for cynicism; and is abundant in love, quick to forgive, compassionate, and trusting. Jesus is saying that the faith of children isn't just to be applauded but replicated.

The disciples themselves may well have been young people. We know they were mostly young men; in the case of the fishermen, many commentators believe they were teenagers at the time Jesus called them. It's a little bit of a stretch to say that, as a result, Jesus was the first youth worker, but it is true to say that He believed in young people, He invested in them, and over the course of three years apprenticed them to the point at which He was happy to leave them in charge of the master plan to build His church.

In the Old Testament, there seems to be no line or distinction drawn between God's young and old followers either. For the people of Israel, family life revolved around God – everyone in the family unit was on the journey of learning the Scriptures, understanding the sacrificial system, and perhaps most importantly understanding the grand story of Israel's relationship with God. Parents invested in bringing up children to receive the faith that they carried (see Psalm 78:1–8); they would look forward to annual camping trips on which they would stay together in "Succoth huts" (see Leviticus 23:34–43). The week-long Feast of Tabernacles wouldn't have been a dull duty but a highlight of the family's year, as for seven days all Israel would celebrate together the stories of what God had done for them. Children weren't on the outside, but rather at the centre of this and other festivals. When God tells "all Israel" to come together, He isn't just talking about the adults.

What does all this mean for us now? It means that whether or not we choose to invest in young people is not a question of rota capacity or our own personal vision. It's a question of obedience to God. There is no group of people that God isn't interested in.

In fact, He seems to show a particular passion at times for our investment in the next generation. We do youth work because God loves young people.

A lost generation?

Newspaper headlines are dangerous things. Not only do they report the news; in many cases they reinforce or even create it. A good example of this, with which certain sections of the media are obsessed, is house prices. In the UK over the last quarter of a century, house prices have risen so fast, so totally out of proportion with earnings and basic common sense, that many people who might have expected to be able to afford a home find themselves unable to clutch at even the bottom rung of the "housing ladder". At the same time, certain newspapers have found this subject enthralling enough to devote a huge and uneven proportion of their annual front-page space to talking about it. "House Prices Rocketing Again" was a familiar sight throughout the 1990s and early 2000s; "Home Market to Crash" is a more recent stuck-record example. In both cases the prophecies have usually proved accurate. Of course they have. Greedy (in boom times) or desperate (more recently) estate agents have used these headlines – and the sense of public confidence or lack thereof that they create – to manage sales, and either inflate prices (leading to that unnatural growth curve) or generate price cuts from worried sellers. The newspaper headlines (which most of us see, even if we don't read the newspapers themselves) play a huge part in setting the mood of a nation on a range of subjects. One of these is young people.

Negative headlines about young people have abounded for the last decade. A generation of teenagers have been demonized as malicious "hoodies" who deliberately congregate in intimidating packs. By reporting the negative and regrettable actions of a few young people, and by using emotive language like "feral", "yobs", and "thugs", the same newspaper front pages that have caused house prices to rise and fall have stigmatized and stereotyped an entire generation. In reaction, the readers of those papers, indoctrinated by a potent mix of loaded reporting, prejudice, and the all-important sliver of truth (because some young people do behave horribly), subtly change their behaviour and attitudes towards young people. They cross the street when they see a teenager in a hoody, unaware that in all probability they're avoiding a fourteen-year-old girl returning home from a cold hockey practice. While as a society we still cherish our children, we've begun to develop a fear of our teenagers.

This fear, this act of crossing-the-street-to-avoid, does not go unnoticed by the teenagers themselves. They are developing a corporate sense of rejection, fuelled not only by the newspaper headlines and the regrettable actions of a few, but also by factors such as rising youth unemployment and the spiralling costs of further education. More than rejected, they feel let down, abandoned even – as a group they are not confident that their future is brighter than their present; not since the 1980s has a generation had to live in a context of depressed hope.

And this, of course, is where the church comes in. This is where we have something prophetic, practical, and powerful to say to young people. That there *is* hope – for them and for the world; that they are valuable and valued, both by us and infinitely more by the real and living God. Never has a generation needed good news more than this one. We don't just have an opportunity to share it with them; I believe we have a responsibility to do so. God loves young people; the world has rejected them. Which side of that equation do you think we should be on?

The church needs a future

During seven years as editor of *Youthwork* magazine, I was occasionally asked to be a guest on "Inspirational Breakfast", the flagship morning show on the London-based Premier Christian Radio, with whom *Youthwork* shared offices and a parent media group. An early show meant an early start, and I'll admit to occasionally being grumpy during these interviews as a result.

One such morning, the topic of the live phone-in was set around my appearance on the show; something like: "Why your church should be doing more youth work." The idea was that we would take calls from Christians who wanted to start a youth-work project but didn't know where to start (sound familiar?), and I would give some basic advice from my limited fount of wisdom. The host was enthusiastic about the subject, and gave it an impassioned introduction. The interview began, and we were excited to see the red lights of the phone system lighting up – a sign that people were engaging with the topic and were calling in with their questions. The host put the first caller on air. Let's call her Doreen.

"Good morning, Doreen," said the host. "What's your question for Martin?"

"Oh, I don't want to talk to Martin," replied Doreen briskly. "I just wanted to wish my amazing pastor (let's call him Pastor Phil) a very happy birthday."

Fair enough. Pastor Phil was a very influential figure in the London church; it was his birthday; Doreen was a fan. An amusing blip.

Or rather, not. Because the next caller was also ringing with birthday wishes for Pastor Phil. And the next one. And the next. The minutes ticked by, and as hard as the host and I tried to sound interesting about youth ministry, the eulogistic birthday greetings just kept coming. There were no callers who wanted to talk about young people and the church. Not any.

Five minutes from the end of my slot, I lost it. After what must have been the twentieth straight call from a member of Pastor Phil's congregation (I still swear he put them up to it), I grabbed the microphone and pretty much yelled:

"We've had an hour of this phone-in about youth work, and not one person has actually wanted to talk about youth work. Well let me tell you something: if you people (I shouldn't have said 'you people') don't start sitting up and thinking seriously about reaching young people, then in fifty years time you won't have a church at all. And then where will your precious Pastor Phil be?" (I shouldn't have said "precious Pastor Phil" either).

I like to revise history in my head so that I slammed something on the desk and stormed out in disgust at the indifference of the London church. Actually we cut to the travel news, and then I apologized for getting so hot and bothered. Yet my point, however unhelpfully I might have expressed it, still stands. All the statistics tell us that, over the last hundred years, the church has been managing steady decline. At the turn of the twentieth century, there were around 9 million children and teenagers in church each week in the UK.[1] Adult attendance was an entrenched part of British and American culture. The numbers haven't just sunk, they've plummeted, and one of the few rays of hope in recent years has been the growth and influence of youth ministry. Statistics from the UK organization Christian Research clearly demonstrate that the churches that are growing in number are generally those which also invest in youth and children's ministry. Those that don't (around 50 per cent of churches, according to the same survey), aren't growing at all.[2]

Simply put, if we want the church to have a future, then we have to commit to intentionally passing the baton of faith on to the next and future generations. We have to help young people to understand that they can take an active part in the church; we

---

1   Source: Evangelical Alliance Council meeting, March 2012.
2   *Pulling Out of the Nosedive* by Peter Brierley (Christian Research, 2006).

have to create a church in which they will feel comfortable and wanted. If we have no young people, then we have no heirs. We can't simply hold on to the hope that people will drift through the doors of our churches in later life. And if a church has no young people, and holds no desire to get some, then it should probably start thinking about putting its affairs in order. Those old buildings would be perfect as a chain of trendy wine bars, what with all that cool stonework and those beautiful windows. Ironically, they'll be full of young people again.

The church needs a present

It's only half the story to suggest that we should be motivated by our desire to ensure that the church has a future. That is of course important, and as we look at our place in 2,000 years of church growth we should feel no small sense of responsibility. This message of protecting the future of the congregation is often the most persuasive when we're talking to church leaders and other church members, but it should not be allowed to drown out the imperative to see young people not only as the church of tomorrow, but also as the church of today.

Andy Hickford's landmark 1998 book *Essential Youth* was originally subtitled "Why your church needs young people". The answer to that wasn't that they will continue to ensure that the buildings are full when the present generation has died out – although as his starting point Hickford admits that he used to be motivated by exactly that outcome – but that they provide our best chance of effectively reaching and discipling those outside the church. As he says in his introduction:

Today's church is really struggling with contemporary culture, yet it has in its midst people who belong to that culture and who can be employed in helping the church engage that culture. These people are the youth of

our churches. The world needs them. The church needs them, and for
everybody's sake we need them now.[3]

Hickford's book – which was published just as youth ministry in
the UK was starting to be taken much more seriously by the church
– casts young people as cultural experts, able to translate between
church and world. He argues that, for the good of its continued
health, growth, and activism, the church must take young people
to its heart, not seeking merely to entertain or keep hold of them,
but allowing them to play an active, even leading role in ministry
and mission.

The metaphor might seem a little dated now, but Hickford's
central idea, that young people are an invaluable resource for the
church because they see through the same "cultural specs" as much of
the world they live in, still holds true. Teenagers have a much better
radar for cultural relevance than those of us in the generations above
them. To create an expression of Christian community that seeks
to involve and attract young people, without actually consulting or
involving any young people in that process, is a bit like asking an
Uzbekistani man for directions without any sort of phrasebook or
interpreter. You can vaguely attempt to head the way he pointed,
but ultimately you've not been equipped for the journey because you
didn't understand the language it was explained in.

We need young people in our churches, then, not simply
because we want those buildings to be full in the future, but
because we have a vision for a more vibrant, effective, and attractive
church today. Properly equipped and mentored, young people can
become effective leaders while they're still young. They can be given
opportunities to unleash often-immense musical gifts; they can play
practically any role in the context of a church "service" (theological
and denominational boundaries permitting); they can be an asset to
the life of the church in countless ways. So don't for a moment think

3   Andy Hickford, *Essential Youth* (Kingsway, 1998), p. 12.

of teenagers as that group of people who occupy the back two rows of the evening service with faces wiped of life by catatonic boredom; if you want, they can practically run the place. And just think what might happen, and who might begin to come along, if they did…

Further reading...

Essential Youth (2nd edition) – Andy Hickford, Authentic, 2004
No Ceiling to Hope – Patrick Regan and Liza Hoeksma, Monarch, 2012

2

Listen

Successful youth ministry starts in prayer.

That's not to say that much can't be achieved under our own steam, that we can't make a big impact on a community without giving God a second thought. Many people do.

Yet if we want to be involved in youth work that is truly transformational, that brings about lasting change in individuals and communities through a realization of the love and power of God – if that is our aspiration, then we need to begin on our knees.

That might seem like a really obvious thing to say, but I've lost count of the number of times when, in my own work with teenagers, I have found myself rather taking God for granted. Weeks spent planning an event, and then a hasty prayer on the night itself; hours of planning ploughed into making a youth talk as funny and impactful as possible, and then a sudden realization just as I'm about to walk on stage that I should probably have involved God in this process. In His immense grace, so often I find He blesses the work anyway – but this is not the way it should be. God should be recognized in the genesis of things (no pun intended); right at the start of a "new thing", the pioneers must pray.

In 2009, I was incredibly privileged to be part of a group of youth workers who came from across the country to gather in Bridgend, South Wales. At the time there had been a string of high-profile suicides among teenagers and young adults in the area, a worrying trend that was way out of sync with the national average. In the middle of the town, a Christian youth centre had become a focal point both for an extraordinary band of local youth workers and for worried teenagers, many of whom were having to cope with the grief of losing friends two or three times over.

I have never been the sort of person to hear the voice of God clearly, but on this occasion I had an unusual certainty about what He was saying. The UK youth-ministry community had to gather in Bridgend. With zero publicity and zero budget, I called and emailed every friend in youth work I had with a simple message: a date and a time to gather in this town (which for most of my friends in the south-east of England was not a short journey away) to pray. A couple of weeks later, over fifty of us showed up in that youth centre: none of us quite sure what to do to make the situation better; all of us armed only with a willingness – or even a desperation – to seek God.

In the early afternoon a few of us took turns to pray for individual youth workers who'd had to cope with the awful consequences of the suicides. Some were concerned about a "domino effect" within friendship groups; others worried that there was something deeply wrong on a spiritual level. Praying from a position of complete ignorance was actually quite liberating. We had no expertise or deep words of advice to bring; we could only beg God to intervene.

Later on a group of around 100 people – half local, half of us visiting – walked together to a nearby church. With a very loose structure planned for a service together, we sang a few songs, a few of the local people shared their stories of living through the suicides, and then we began to pray. I will never forget the hour that followed, as men and women, young and old, wept, and worshipped, and grieved, and cried out in hope. We were united both by our passion for God and by the love He had given us for this generation. We prayed for an end to the suicides; we prayed for strength for those working with young people locally – both inside and outside the church. Armed with none of the answers, we earnestly sought God together, and the sense of His presence at that moment was like nothing I have experienced since.

In the weeks and months that followed, I received several pieces of good news from my contact in that town. First and foremost, the wave of young people taking their own lives appeared to have come to an end. Excitingly, a Christian mission to the town had seen many young people make a decision to begin following Jesus. Encouragingly, many of the youth leaders – and their respective churches – had begun to work together in a more joined-up way. Out of the still-painful ashes of tragedy, some green shoots of hope were beginning to emerge.

Our presence in Bridgend that day didn't change things. We might have been a source of encouragement, but none of those remarkable results could be attributed to anything that we did. God, however, has the power to change everything, and His presence in that meeting might just have been the catalyst for the good things that followed. As I reflect on it now, it seems to me that there is something very poignant, very powerful even, about Christians coming together and admitting before God: "We don't know what to do; please help."

That, I believe, should be the starting position in youth ministry. The people of God holding their hands up and realizing not only their limitations, but also the boundless, limitless potential of that God to change the world for the better. He will use us to accomplish incredible things, when we first adopt a position of surrender.

Prayer in practice

Before anything else, then, you should look to commit some significant time to praying for the "new thing". For you, the leader, this means an investment of daily time with God, but it is also powerful to gather several people together to pray and listen corporately to God ("for where two or three gather in my name" says Jesus in Matthew 18:20, "there I am with them").

On an individual level, I would suggest that you set aside a period of time (it could be a week, could be a month or forty days) to seek God using a number of the spiritual disciplines. The disciplines are ancient Christian practices, activities within our own strength, which draw us close to God and open us up to His infinitely greater power (for much more detail on this, and resources for teaching these incredible practices to young people, see my book *The Beautiful Disciplines*). The first and most important of these is prayer; it is the practice that underpins the rest of the spiritual disciplines. Prayer can take many, many forms; in fact the main reason why many people find a regular prayer life so difficult is that they have such a limited view of what it is. For some personality types, long periods of speaking out loud or reciting a long internal monologue are difficult activities for which they don't have the concentration or the words. Yet that is only one form of prayer; in modern culture we have invented hundreds of ways to communicate with one another – so why do we so often limit ourselves to one form of communication when it comes to talking to God?

Drawing pictures, writing an email, scribbling sticky notes and pinning them to a noticeboard: all of these are valid forms of prayer – all messages that our omniscient God can read and answer. All that we should be wary of is that those prayers aren't just one-way traffic; we must understand prayer as a live, two-way conversation. In Matthew 7, Jesus explains the "Ask, Seek, Knock" principle – prayers aren't just sent into a vacuum; they are received messages, and God answers them. If we're asking for guidance, wisdom, and discernment, we should also be prepared to receive some of them directly.

Another of the spiritual disciplines that we might use during this period is fasting. Up to about 200 years ago, the practice of going without food in order to focus one's mind on God was as central to Western Christianity as prayer and corporate worship. Yet, perhaps because it is the element that requires the most self-sacrifice, it has been somewhat downgraded within church culture. We need only look to Jesus to see how important He thought fasting was: a superhuman effort of forty days without food preceded an extraordinary three years of ministry. Right there in Luke 4 we read that He left His period of fasting and temptation and "returned to Galilee in the power of the Spirit, and news about him spread through the whole countryside" (verse 14). There is something about fasting that unleashes the power of God.

The forty-day food fast that Jesus practised was truly supernatural, and should not be attempted – the human body is unlikely to survive much more than thirty days without food. Instead, we might build the practice of fasting into our everyday life. Perhaps you miss a meal every day for a week – using that time instead for prayer and Bible reading. Alternatively, you might want to set aside one whole day as a fast day, taking yourself away on a twenty-four-hour retreat to pray and listen to God while you deny yourself food. Fasting itself is a little uncomfortable, but it is amazing both how that discomfort focuses the mind, and how God seems to respond with visions, guidance, and an outpouring of his Holy Spirit when we do.

One more discipline you might like to consider during this period is solitude. This is the practice of taking ourselves out of normal circulation, finding a place where we will not be disturbed, and listening for the still, small voice of God. As Jesus' own ministry intensified, we read in the Gospels that He "often withdrew to lonely places and prayed" (Luke 5:16). Jesus didn't just take a few moments in the midst of His busy schedule to utter a quick prayer for help; He deliberately retreated, even during periods of intense activity, to secret places where He wouldn't be disturbed. He knew that the energy he needed was sourced from spending time with His Father. In the same way, spending time in those "lonely places" with only our heavenly Father will energize and envision us for the mission ahead.

For some of us the idea of silence is scary, and intensely counter-cultural. We live, after all, in a culture that moves at breakneck speed; our minds are constantly bombarded with words, sounds, images, and media that chip away at our attention span and condition us for constant multi-tasking. The idea of doing one thing at a time is sometimes a stretch; the idea of doing nothing at all is positively alien. Even for extroverts like myself (for Myers–Briggs fans, I'm an off-the-scale "E"), the discipline of solitude is thankfully something that we can train ourselves in. I wouldn't suggest, for instance, that a person uninitiated in the practice of silent reflection dives into the deep end of a three-day silent retreat, although, even for extroverts, this is perfectly achievable after a while. At first, then, you might try to spend twenty minutes a day in silence, upping the length of time as and when these periods of quiet become more natural.

So what do you do during these moments of solitude? It's not strictly true that this discipline requires us to do absolutely nothing. To blur the lines with another discipline, meditation, we might use some of this time to reflect on God, on our own journey of faith, and on the local community that we seek to serve. Strictly speaking, however, the discipline of solitude is about clearing our thoughts to make room for God. Clearing one's mind is an active, not a passive, process. Whenever we attempt to stop thinking about our usual interests or concerns, a thousand other ideas, memories, and observations see their opportunity to rush in and grab brain space. So, as we focus on God, we have to work quite hard – to begin with at least – to keep the channel clear.

In these times, we are actively listening to God – a vital pursuit as we try to discern the right course for our youth ministry. This, and the other practices listed above, is as relevant and important when we've been doing youth ministry for ten years as it is when we begin. God's plan is ever-unfolding; to keep in step with it we need to ensure we are continually returning to Him in prayer: putting Him in his rightful place as the centre and the source of all our work, listening for His voice and discerning where He is at work, calling us to join in as His fellow workers.

Listening to your community

Alongside the process of listening to God's voice, we should also commit significant time and effort to listening to the local community that we seek to serve. God, who works in all things, is as likely to speak to us through this process as through times of silent reflection, so both are crucially important as we seek to start something new.

Listening to a community involves two processes: our own observation, and personal interviews. The first stage, observation, is what we and our fellow leaders discern about the specific needs and challenges of the local context. The second, interviewing, is where we gather knowledge and data from real, live, local young people! It might be, for instance, that you are looking to start a youth project in a rural area, as a collaboration between three small churches; it might be that a city-centre church has charged you with getting a drop-in youth club started right in the midst of a densely populated area. Each of these contexts will be very different from any other place, in their own ways unique, and we should do all we can to understand that uniqueness *before* we start.

Wherever you are planning to work, there will be **geographical** issues to consider – for instance, do the young people in your community or (for want of a better word) "catchment area" live close together in urban estates, or spaced apart in villages and hamlets? Is open space at a premium or abundantly available; are local transport links tricky or straightforward? There will also be **social** issues to understand, as you analyse the sorts of homes and backgrounds the young people in your area come from. Some areas are very affluent, others much less so, and more often than not a community will have a real mix of rich and poor, although one or the other of these might not be immediately obvious.

Alongside this, you should take steps to understand the **cultural** make-up of your community. Is your town's population 98 per cent Caucasian, or 50 per cent Bengali? Is there a large Polish Catholic community, or a significant proportion of young people from Muslim homes? This data is vital if you are going to create youth work that truly seeks to meet local needs.

There is no one youth culture. Rather, there are diverse **youth cultures**, tribes of young people which are divided (usually quite peacefully) along lines of interest, fashion, and (don't underestimate this one) musical taste. Through both observation and interview, you should be able to build up a good picture of what kinds of groupings exist locally. This information is vital: if there is a huge Goth culture in your town, it might not be right to launch that acoustic folk open-mic night you've been planning. Understanding which youth cultures are represented locally will give you a helpful lead on the kinds of service you might want to provide.

There will be other questions to ask. There is little point in creating duplicate or competitive initiatives – in most areas there are precious few low-cost activities aimed at teenagers, so don't make them choose. So if there is a local boys' club that runs brilliant football coaching, don't launch a boys' five-a-side league. Similarly, if there is a good Christian youth club in your town on Thursday nights, don't set up a direct rival. Instead, take time during this early stage to find out what provision is already made for young people locally, through the local church (the biggest provider of voluntary youth services in the UK and many other countries), through statutory bodies, and by other local providers. In doing this, you will begin to get a picture of where the gaps are.

Community observation form

You will have various sources for the information you gather. Use the headings below as space to record your various findings – then use the completed form as a resource to help you plan your youth work project.

What are the geographical opportunities and challenges in your area?

E.g. Young people live close together / spread out? Natural locations for meetings/activities?

_____

_____

_____

_____

What is the social make-up of your community?

Are the young people in your area affluent and time-poor, or do they come from homes that are generally struggling on low incomes? Are different areas of your community home to different socio-economic groups?

_____

_____

_____

_____

What cultures, ethnicities, and religions are represented locally?

_____

_____

_____

_____

What evidence of different youth cultures do you see?

Are there obvious local groupings delineated by musical or other interests?

_____

_____

_____

_____

What provision already exists for young people locally?

E.g. open youth clubs, extended school activities, sports activities, uniformed organizations, skate park, alcohol-free club nights, etc.

_____

_____

_____

_____

What do other churches in your area offer for young people?

_____

_____

_____

_____

Additional comments/reflections

_____

_____

_____

_____

To continue this thought, your interview process should seek to identify what kind of youth provision local young people would choose if they were given the option. Not only will this potentially prevent you from creating a project that no one actually wants, meeting a need that isn't really there, but also it could throw up ideas that you'd never have thought of yourself.

Interviews should be carried out with at least two DBS-checked adults present,[4] and you will probably want to interview several young people at a time. If there are young people connected with your church through family (even if they don't have a faith), these are your first point of call; you might also ask them to invite other friends from school or their local area to come with them. Ideally you'd speak to at least ten young people from an appropriately diverse range of cultures and social backgrounds. This process could be carried out as an electronic survey, but I would recommend face-to-face interviews; you could make use of the form on the next page, but you might want to amend this with your own questions. Don't worry about processing the data you collect at this point; we'll deal with that in another chapter.

The interview process itself could provide a great point of first contact with young people in your community. Those you have spoken to will at least be intrigued by what you decide to launch as a result of your consultations, and will naturally be more likely to buy in to the concept.

---

4   In the UK, everyone working with under-eighteens in either a formal or informal educational environment (such as youth work) should be subject to a Disclosure and Barring Service (DBS) check for each context in which they work with under-eighteens. This means that if they are already DBS-checked as a school teacher, they will still need a separate disclosure to do youth work.

The process normally takes a couple of weeks, and at time of writing costs £26 per standard disclosure, (£44 for an enhanced one). In the vast majority of cases, these disclosure reports will come back clear; for more information, and for advice on what to do if an issue arises from a DBS check, visit the Churches' Child Protection Advisory Service (CCPAS) at www.ccpas.co.uk, or contact them on 0845 120 45 50. And while making sure you have procured up-to-date DBS checks, don't forget to submit your own application!

If you are reading this in a country other than the UK, make sure you find out the legal requirements in your area.

A few years ago, I was asked by the leadership of the small church I attended to start a new youth group. There were a handful of teenagers around – all of them coming along on a Sunday because their parents did, and a few more in the orbit of the church who hadn't been on the premises for a while. The night the pastor enlisted me, I returned home giddy with grand ideas. We'd have a sports evening for the football-obsessed lads, a community action project on the local estate to appease the social activists, and a small worship meeting which would doubtless grow into a youth congregation within months. Then, thankfully, I decided to meet some of the young people involved, just to gather a few opinions on my brilliant ideas.

I'm thankful I did. The "football-mad" lads I had observed turned out to be quite sick of a diet of non-stop football. The idea of going on to that estate was daunting for several of them, because of family and other relationship issues I hadn't known about it. And half of them hated singing! Had I ploughed ahead with my own ideas, I'd have created a group for me, not them. Their ideas turned out to be far less grand: a weekly meeting in my front room, where they wouldn't be under the gaze of parents or church leaders, and where they could ask anything. We ran it just as they had planned, and for the next two years almost every young person on our "hit list" came along every single week. They had shaped it. They owned it. They committed to it. All because, by the grace of God, I remembered to listen to them.

Further reading...

Celebration of Discipline (new edition) – Richard Foster, Hodder & Stoughton, 2008
The Beautiful Disciplines – Martin Saunders, Monarch, 2011

Interview form

Use one form per interview – but you may want to interview several subjects at the same time.

What kinds of things do you enjoy doing outside school and your own home?

You may need to prompt with some relevant local examples of activities, clubs etc.

_____

_____

_____

_____

What's missing for your age group locally?

Again, you may need to prompt with ideas – but give the subjects a chance to think.

_____

_____

_____

_____

Tell me a bit about your taste in music – what was the last album you downloaded and loved?

Supplementary: do you enjoy / attend live music events? If so, what kinds?

_____

_____

_____

What would you want from a youth worker? Would that sort of person be useful to you?

Supplementary: If so, how? If not, why not?

_____

_____

_____

Do you believe in God? How important is that question to you?

Supplementary: What's your view on the church – generally, and specifically (the one you represent)?

_____

_____

_____

[Depending on answer to previous question]

Are you interested in exploring issues to do with spirituality and faith?

Supplementary: If so, how would you want to do that?

_____

_____

_____

Additional comments/reflections

_____

_____

_____

_____

3

Team First

One of the most brilliant things about Jesus' ministry on earth; one of the things that sets Him apart from other religious figures and which gives His story a resounding ring of authenticity, is that He led a team. Unlike many leaders who have since sought to emulate Him, He wasn't a lone ranger; He didn't travel from town to town with a tent and a miracle cure. He might inevitably have been the star attraction, but He constantly pushed others into the limelight, and He invested heavily in those He had chosen to help and succeed Him. History records few leaders, certainly in the ancient world, who led in this way; yet one of the key reasons for the church's phenomenal growth from a handful of rebels to an estimated figure of two billion was that Jesus built a team. Incredibly, Jesus made sure His ministry wasn't dependent on His always being around. This is a sobering challenge to anyone who might seek to have a "ministry" today.

Youth ministry built on a single personality (who isn't Jesus) always fails in the end. If a group of young people begin to see a single youth worker as some sort of charismatic high priest between them and God, then ultimately their faith will be placed in the wrong person. (This isn't just a problem for groups with only one leader; it can also be evident when one leader among many becomes the dominant "star attraction".) Instead, youth ministry should always take a team approach, although this can take many forms. In this chapter we'll look at different shapes that teams might take; how to recruit, manage, and look after a group of volunteers, and how you might then work together to achieve your aims.

Team shapes

Youth-work teams can take many forms, in part dependent on the kind of youth work you are looking to deliver. A mainly schools-based team, for instance, might look very different from a team running an open youth club, which would look very different again from a team of youth cell leaders. Although to some degree the team will inevitably be shaped by the people who volunteer, it is a good idea to think about what kind of team you might want before you set out to recruit them.

For simplicity's sake, we will assume that you are a solitary volunteer youth worker, aiming to recruit a team of further volunteers. Although at this stage we begin to play a game of egg and chicken, you will probably have some initial thoughts on:

- How many volunteers you might realistically look to recruit.

- How many volunteers you need as an absolute minimum (technically this is at least one more than you – for the sake of safeguarding and best practice)

- Which areas of leadership you feel less confident in, or feel you need help with (for instance, you may not be an up-the-front person, but you might be a brilliant organizer)

- What kinds and mix of skills you're hoping to get on your team.

With these thoughts in mind, you can then begin the process of recruiting volunteers – on which, more shortly.

Your defined "youth-work team" doesn't have to stop with the group of hands-on volunteers who are actually going to deliver the youth work. There are also other key people whom you might want to see – and communicate with – as part of your wider "team".

I would humbly yet strongly recommend that you consider formally organizing people to pray for your youth work. There may be those in your church, for instance, who are passionate about positive engagement with young people, but who do not feel they have the skills, time, or confidence to get involved in the hands-on stuff. Why not ask them to commit to praying regularly for your work? Recruiting people who are prepared to bring your work before God on a regular basis can be a vital element of successful youth ministry. Make sure that you keep them regularly updated (for instance with a weekly email), so that they both feel involved and have specific issues, concerns, or pieces of good news to pray about.

Your wider "team" might also involve people who help you in an advisory role. There may be youth workers at other churches, or local denominational youth advisers, who are able to help you think through your developing youth-work project. In addition, there may be individuals with specific skills in your church who, while they are unable to commit to regular hands-on involvement, have much to offer when it comes to helping you to think through and plan the youth work. I know for instance of a church in which a highly skilled and extremely time-pressed business consultant, also a church member, gives a small amount of his time each month to applying his consultancy skills to the church youth work. This is brief but invaluable input for the youth worker involved, and creates an opportunity for an enthusiastic person with very limited time.

All this is to say: teams come in all shapes and sizes – don't feel that there is a certain winning formula to which you have to adhere. The most important question to ask is simply: what kind of team does this youth work need? Once you have an answer to that question, you can begin the business of recruitment…

Volunteers

An announcement from the front at a church service is one of the best opportunities through which to recruit people to join you in your work with young people. Your challenge, then, is to create a memorable, compelling notice. Your message – that youth-ministry volunteering is just about the best, most rewarding, and most important way a church member might spend their time – has to get under the skin of those listening if you're going to persuade them to volunteer.

As I write, I've just witnessed a brilliant example of such an announcement, from our church's now – sadly – former youth and children's minister. It went something like this:

"We are so excited about the youth work here at the church – but we also believe that we are only scratching the surface of what could be achieved. We believe that there is so much that God wants to do, and we are seeing opportunities open up in local schools and other places, but we just don't have the manpower to do everything that we would like to do.

"Do you think you could invest a little of your time in helping with the youth work? Could you run a group, or just help out occasionally? What we'd love to do is find things that you're passionate about, that could increase our work with young people. So, if you're excited about sport, or about the Bible, or about praying, or about feeding the homeless, or about music… we can use you. We'd love to talk to you. Help us to do even more than we're currently doing."

Now, of course, this one speech was perfect for one specific church at one specific time. I'm not for one moment suggesting you read this out verbatim. But there are some helpful principles within it that form a good model for an address to potential volunteers. Opening positively, he sets out the vision for what could be

– mentioning new, live opportunities in the community, and clarifying a sense of God-ordained purpose. He then makes the opportunity real, stressing a limited time commitment, and then earthing it in the potential volunteers' existing interests. He finishes with a direct call to action, which feels achievable. It's a great piece of communication, and so it proved, because afterwards several volunteers came forward.

Actually, though, there was a second part to the address. Having outlined the need, he then invited a young person – one on whose life the work of the youth-ministry team at the church has had a remarkable impact – to share some of her story of what it's actually like to be part of the youth group. She grabbed the opportunity with both hands, brilliantly demonstrating exactly why the youth worker had just spoken so passionately about the need for resources. This combination of attention-grabbing plea and compelling human evidence would have convinced even the most hard-nosed church member that this area of ministry was important.

If you're starting literally from scratch, you won't have testimonies like this to draw on. It may be possible, however, to use the voice of a young person from a nearby church who – with their youth leader – may be able to speak convincingly on the benefits of church-based youth workers (most of the youth workers I know would be thrilled to answer such a need – apart from anything it presents a great opportunity for the young person).

This isn't the only way to recruit volunteers, but it is an important one if you're seeking to draw them from within a church family. Whether this creates a pool of interested people or not, you should also look to approach people individually who you feel might be a good "fit" for the initiative (naturally, you should pray about this first). Crucially, you're not actually offering them a role – you're simply inviting them to be part of a further conversation with you – more on this in a moment. To make the whole thing more tangible, you might share a little of your vision for the youth work, and where you see that tallying with their skill set; you might also want to talk in terms of a tangible time commitment – say twelve months. An open-ended proposition is much more daunting than a fixed-term one.

Other routes for recruitment might be through a church notice sheet, or through a network of house or cell groups. For each method of communication, the style of message used above is still applicable: sharing vision, and then making the opportunity tangible and manageable.

Once you have a pool (let's think positively here!) of volunteers, it isn't just a case of putting them to work. You can't just send any group of sane adults into a room with teenagers, and expect a thriving youth ministry. Through meeting each potential volunteer individually for an initial conversation – and making no promises about the outcome – you need to establish whether this person is a positive and responsible addition to your team. You may want to base some questions on the following areas of discussion:

- Does the person have any experience of working with young people, and what did this entail?

- What skills, interests, and expertise do they bring?

- Why do they want to get involved? (There is no one right answer to this, but there are a few wrong ones…)

- Do they have a faith – and what does that look like in practice?

That last point is really important, by the way. When I think back to my own time in a Christian youth group, as a podgy teenager with unmanageable hair and a growth spurt that seemed to get deferred every year, I can't really remember anything that I was taught. I don't remember what my leaders said to me, but I do remember in fairly clear detail how they lived their lives.

Most of them were volunteers holding down full-time jobs; many of them had families too. They might have been time-pressed, but that didn't stop them from having Christlike characters. They loved Jesus and, regardless of what they were trying to tell us to do, they were working in their own lives to be more like Him. This was formative for me – I wasn't hugely interested in most of what my leaders were teaching us, but I was sure that, when I grew up, I wanted to be like them.

Volunteer youth leaders are role models whether they like it or not; it's important we choose people to work alongside us who will be a positive influence on young people. The ability to drive a minibus or run a tuck shop is valuable, but that's really not the most important qualifier for a good youth-work volunteer. The first and most important thing to assess when you are meeting a potential youth-work volunteer is their character.

If you feel happy to proceed after this meeting (and that shouldn't be a foregone conclusion: some people are not going to make great youth-work volunteers and with diplomacy and discernment this will be the moment to tell them), then you can invite them to help you with the youth work (subject to DBS clearance, see note on page 30).

Working together, keeping them, and keeping them happy

Let's assume at this point that you now have some sort of volunteer team.

The first, and most important, thing to remember now is this: in youth work, volunteers are your most precious resource. You're here to serve the young people, but you simply won't be able to do it for very long without the commitment and sacrifice of your volunteers. Many experienced youth workers invest as much as a third of their total working week in their adult volunteers. If that sounds like a poor use of time, think again – once a youth ministry reaches a certain size, a well-managed volunteer team capable of a degree of autonomy becomes critical. If all you've built is a rota, what happens when you need to deal with two crises at once? Managing volunteers doesn't mean handing out a list of jobs; it means building a team and growing others in leadership.

With all this in mind, here's an outline of some of the things you'll want to consider in maintaining a healthy and successful volunteer team:

Get together – and not just to pray

You'll create a sense of team cohesion by getting that team together regularly. And while it is important that you spend time praying for the young people, for your community, and for the unfolding vision, don't let that be the only reason you gather. Build a social evening into your programme every term, and make sure your Christmas party makes the rest of the church wish they'd volunteered too!

Value people

My vicar, Revd Phil Andrew, has an amazing gift for remembering names. Legend has it that his first appearance on the church scene was at a barbecue a couple of weeks before he was due to be installed. He stood at the entrance, and introduced himself to every single person, asking them for their name in return. The following day, when he made his first appearance at a church service, he greeted everyone by name, and by all accounts he barely got one wrong. Almost instantly, the congregation decided that they liked him.

This story illustrates two things. Firstly, that Phil Andrew missed his calling as a cruise-ship Memory Man, and, secondly, that people feel valued when you take an interest in them. When you're going to be working closely with a team, you'll need to remember more than just their names – so make an effort to find out about their lives; what they're concerned or excited about; what motivates them and makes them tick. Pray for your team members – not just that they'll work well for you, but that God will bless them. If your volunteers feel valued, they're much more likely to stick around for the long term.

Make development part of the deal

You should be upfront from the start with prospective volunteers that you don't see them as the finished article, and that you'll be looking to help them learn and develop as youth leaders. Even with a modest budget, you can organize plenty of input; the key thing here is realizing that development isn't just about you as the main leader. There are high-quality courses in volunteer youth ministry (see the Christian Youth Work Training website for details: www.cywt.org.uk), but you may also find out that your local authority runs training events for youth-work volunteers – just contact them and ask.

There's also a lot of good writing about youth ministry, and you as the leader shouldn't be the only one reading it. Invite your whole team to read *Youthwork* magazine and, if they like it, maybe get them their own copies (this "pass-along" thing might feel like Christian sharing, but it's killing us!); if you can afford it, choose one good book every term, buy a copy for everyone, and read and discuss it together. Investing in continued development will help volunteers to take their role seriously, because they'll see that you're taking it seriously.

If it isn't working out...

Of course, the recruitment process outlined above isn't foolproof, and, even if it were, things invariably don't work out as we expect them to. If you're doing youth ministry for any length of time, you can expect to encounter a problem with one of your volunteers at some point. It's essential that you face this situation with professionalism, prayer, and wisdom, but you shouldn't approach it as a foregone conclusion. Just because it isn't working, doesn't mean it *can't* work. Now clearly there are some problems that do mean the end of the road – a volunteer being violent, or behaving inappropriately with one of the young people, for instance (these may also entail police intervention). There are other less serious issues that will also require you to ask them to leave, for instance if a character problem is having a seriously negative influence on the young people.

A lot of the time, however, what's needed is a moment for both of you to refocus and re-evaluate. Imagine, for instance, that one of your leaders is struggling to act as the adult in group situations, and instead seems to regress into an overgrown teenager (this is quite common – many people get involved in youth ministry as a way of avoiding ever having to leave the youth group!). This certainly isn't a "sackable" offence, but neither do you want it to continue. What you might choose to do in this situation is to organize an informal meeting with the person involved, and work through a few questions, such as:

- How do they feel the youth work is going, and how do they feel about their role within it?

- How comfortable do they feel when leading a small group of young people? What challenges does this present for them?

- How do they think they can improve as a youth leader?
  What might be areas of weakness that they have identified in themselves?

Obviously the questions will differ depending on the situation, but an honest discussion along these lines is a great way to provoke a natural course correction. If it's clear that isn't working, you will need to be more directive, and before the end of the meeting challenge the person lovingly (and biblically) about their behaviour.

To help deal with these kinds of challenges pre-emptively, you might consider introducing annual informal "appraisals" with your volunteers, where you meet one to one and talk through these questions and more, and agree together where you'd like to grow to in a year's time. This may feel wrong for your context/team, however.

Sometimes a volunteer will decide that they've had enough, and in these situations I would always advise you not to beg them to reconsider. The temptation – especially if you already have a small team – will always be to try to talk them round, but in my experience this never ends well. If you succeed, you'll simply end up with a person on your team who feels frustrated and guilty. If they want to go, let them go, and get back on that recruitment merry-go-round!

Dream team

There's a reason why teams have been given such prominence in this book: without the support of others, you will not be effective in youth ministry. More than that, if you don't manage to take the hearts and minds of your team with you as you lead, then you are heading for trouble. Strong youth-work projects begin with the building of a team, and flourish through the good leadership of that team.

One of my best experiences in youth work was my first – as a volunteer in a large team. The model was great (for that context): we would hold a Sunday-evening youth congregation, and then a social café-style event afterwards. The committed Christian young people came to the first half; their friends who didn't have a faith joined us for the second. More often than not, a handful of the second group arrived early enough to catch some of the "service"; wonderfully, over time, the two groups became more and more integrated into one.

When I indicated my interest in being involved, the man heading up the work – let's call him Tom (because it's his real name) – came to my house one evening for an initial chat. Right from that meeting (once he'd established that I was sane, with no previous convictions), Tom made every effort to set out the vision behind the youth project.

He told me a little of the history, was open about times when things had not gone so well, and then outlined his hopes for the future. He was compelling, mainly because he talked so passionately about transforming young lives. He was honest, realistic, and likeable. I knew from that point that I could follow his leadership.

I became a regular volunteer, and quickly felt part of the team. There was a great spirit, and the relationships between the various volunteers worked well because we were all committed to the same vision. Our ideas were listened to (and often implemented); we were given responsibility; we came together regularly outside the youth meetings to pray, plan, and socialize. As a result, the whole team enjoyed working for Tom, and for each other. Not entirely surprisingly, the youth work itself flourished during that period – in hindsight I know that this environment fostered deep discipleship in those young people, a stunning number of whom have gone on to maintain an active faith well into their twenties. I'm convinced that a big part of the reason for this was what they saw modelled by their adult leaders.

Unfortunately, not all teams are quite like this. At around the same time, another church that I know well appointed a new youth worker. Now I don't know the man personally, so I can only speculate from the sidelines, but it was clear he didn't approach team ministry in the same way as Tom. Inheriting a large volunteer team, he arrived at the church with his own clear vision, and set about dismantling all the systems, teams, and programmes that his predecessor had initiated. A fantastic preacher, he refocused a relational ministry around big, weekly events, at which he was the star attraction.

At first, the volunteers were dazzled, and excited to be involved with such an exciting young leader. Yet as time wore on it became clear that team and relationship building were not his strong suits. He emailed the volunteers each week with instructions, rather than meeting them to gain their insights and opinions; he made decisions unilaterally, rather than collaboratively. The ministry was on one level thriving – young people were becoming Christians, and there was a buzz and excitement around the events themselves. Yet it was very clear to the volunteers that this had become the leader's show. At the end of that first year, half of the team decided they'd had enough; some of them had been volunteering for years. The leader could not understand as one after another of them met with him to step down. I hope some of them were brave and honest enough to explain truthfully.

Get your team right, and the rest will follow. Youth ministry is never a one-man show; some of the greatest joy I've experienced in over a decade working with young people hasn't come from working with young people at all. When a team of people come together, united by the twin passions of a love of God and a love of young people, amazing, beautiful things can happen. Get recruiting!

Developing Young Leaders
Pete Wynter

Here's a provocative statement for you: "Every young person has the potential to lead and should be given the opportunity to do so."

John Maxwell, a leadership guru, has a simple definition: "Leadership is Influence." If we believe that, then we are all involved in leading others at some level, influencing both positively and negatively. If a young person chooses to become a Christian then they are in effect signing up to leadership, because Jesus' call on our lives is not only to follow Him, but to become like Him, learn from Him and influence the world with the good news of who He is. It could be argued then that good discipleship is also good leadership development, so maybe you are already beginning to develop young leaders without actually realizing it!

The more intentional we become about developing young leaders, the better we will become at it. And the better we become at it, the more the young people we work with will step up into the exciting adventure of becoming an influencer in our world today. So let's have a look at a couple of key considerations as we set about the task of raising young leaders.

Where do you start?

Always start with character. Increasing the ability and gifting of a young person is important if you want to help them lead, but it is always the character of a young person that gives the foundation for effective leadership development. After asking countless leaders around the UK what they look for in a young leader, the leading answer by a long way is "teachability". If a young person is teachable then they will be ready to learn, keen to question and able to reflect on their experiences. Those skills are essential for any leader, and especially for someone who is just starting out. Take time to teach the young people about great characteristics and qualities of well-known leaders so that they begin to aspire to them in their own lives. You'll quickly be able to spot the ones who respond well and begin to grow in their character. When that happens make sure you take time to personally encourage and inspire them to keep going, whilst simultaneously finding opportunities for them to take an active role in leading. Begin calling them a leader, so they know that is what you are helping them to become, and you'll see them rise to the challenge.

How do I create opportunities for them to lead?

Opportunities don't need to be huge or complex, begin by letting the young people do what bits of what you do. Maybe do it with them initially, but there needs to come a time when you trust them to have a go on their own. There may be the odd failure, it may take more of your time than if you just got it done by yourself, but in the long run it will establish the young person as a confident contributor, and will certainly pave the way to them becoming a better leader. Obvious opportunities include helping with kids groups, leading small groups or discussions, taking the lead in team games and activities, sharing stories or even teaching peers from the front. As they get used to these you could begin to involve young people in the planning and organizing of events, so that they take increasing ownership and see what leadership looks like behind the scenes.

And how do I take it to the next level?

Demonstrate and celebrate young people beginning to lead, and others in the group will probably begin to get involved. Before you know it you can encourage a culture of leadership in your group. Plug into opportunities to give them practical and inspirational training and as they continue to grow, so will their capacity to lead. The shape of your job will slowly become very different – encouraging and releasing others to do what you once did.

The fruit of which will be increased engagement and ownership from the young people, and almost certainly growth in depth and numbers.

It's not just the youth group or church who will benefit from developing more young leaders, but society at large. Imagine a day when the UK is full of practically resourced, godly, characterful leaders in every sphere of society, simply because we set about the task of raising them up in our day-to-day youth work. Go for it!

Pete Wynter is the Executive Director of Onelife, an organization that exists to connect and equip young people and students to become exceptional leaders in every sphere of society. www.onelifeonline.org.uk

Further reading

Simply Strategic Volunteers – Tony Morgan and Tim Stevens, Flagship Church Resources, 2004
Sticky Teams – Larry Osborne, Zondervan, 2010
The Volunteer Revolution: Unleashing the Power of Everybody – Bill Hybels, Zondervan, 2004

4

What?

So you've listened to God, and to your community. You've recruited, vetted, and rallied a team. Now what? What is your youth work actually going to look and feel like? What kind of youth ministry are you creating?

That might seem like a strange question if you're new to youth work, but there are actually many models and ways of serving, informally educating, entertaining, and journeying with young people – and lots more that haven't been invented yet. In their efforts to find relevant ways of sharing God's heart with teenagers, Christians all over the world have devised countless strategies, projects, and programmes. So which of these approaches will you seek to emulate, or how will you break new ground?

In a single town, there might be five or six very different approaches to youth ministry. There might be an open youth club, perhaps run in co-operation with the local council, which seeks to create a safe space for all young people in the area to hang out. Several churches probably run "traditional" youth groups, meeting once a week for programmed discipleship activities, and perhaps again for a more social gathering. One church may run a youth congregation, where young people gather for their own contemporary worship service instead of attending (and possibly at the same time as) adult church. The area may have a detached youth worker, looking to build cold-contact relationships with young people who are coming nowhere near the doorstep of the church. There could be a local schools work trust, working alongside churches to send workers into schools to take assemblies and RE lessons, and offer mentoring services. And there might be something more pioneering: a skate project; a football academy run on Christian principles; a community radio station for young people, overseen by a church.

Does that description excite you? It does me. But… I've misled you. The reality is that the above is somewhat idealistic, especially for a smaller town; the majority of the areas with which I'm familiar don't have anything like this breadth of youth ministry. Yet if our villages, towns, and cities really were filled with a diversity of youth projects like this, what might the response be from this generation?

The point of this chapter is to widen your horizons. Don't let the basic model of youth ministry – a small group of teenagers meeting to work through a programme of activities – be the only one you consider. First, you need to ask yourself some questions…

What do you want to achieve?

Let's start broadly, and narrow down to specifics later. Having listened to the needs of your community, to what God might be saying, and to your own vision, what are the "Big Picture" aims of this new youth work initiative? Take a moment now to write down some initial answers to that question. Some possibilities to prompt your thinking:

• Increasing the number of young people who are engaged with your church

• Establishing a Christian presence among local youth cultures

• Building connections with local schools

• Providing meaningful and diversionary activities for young people who have "nothing to do"

• Discipling the teenage children of your adult church members.

Try to limit yourself to two or three aims – the more specific you're able to be at this start-up stage, the more chance you have of creating something truly dynamic.

Be careful, as you do this, not to confuse "outcomes" with "outputs". We often expend lots of energy on creating stuff, building things, developing programmes, and so on. All of which is good, but these are outputs, not outcomes – and that's what we're interested in here. Outcome aims are powerful statements which *describe change*; they explain how things will be different as a result of your output. "To create a weekly breakfast club for young people in our church hall" is an output; "To move our young people to a place where they can confidently share the Christian gospel with their friends" is an outcome. Outcomes are sometimes hard to measure (we'll return to this theme later in the book), but, if we don't aim for them at the start, we'll end up building a boat that doesn't have a rudder.

Take a look at the aims you've written down. Do you have the basis of a mission statement here? You don't need to commit to that just yet – but you may now want to talk to your team about what you've just articulated. Is this the change you want to see in your local community? What might God be saying about and through this? Praying through your aims, mission, and vision at this pre-launch stage is absolutely vital. It is my experienced and considered opinion that, very often, this exciting, vision-casting stage is so much fun that we often neglect to pray it through properly. So, before you rush ahead, please give this some serious prayer – on your own, and as a team. Don't just speak; again, listen. Allow your course to be corrected by the greatest visionary of all.

What resources do you have?

At this point, you need to do an audit of the resources available to you. You've already begun the first part of this process, in the recruitment of your volunteer team. Hopefully by now you'll have had a chance to get to know them a little better, and while interviewing them you will have learned about their skills and interests. As you think about **human resources**, then, make some notes (in whatever way will be most useful for you to refer to later) about the various skills that the individuals in your team bring. On your list, include both practical skills (can they drive? Can any of them drive a minibus?) and "soft" interpersonal/relational skills (can they build relationships? Can they lead from the front?). Try to make as full a list as possible, and then identify ways in which each of your volunteers can have their God-given gifts and skills put to use.

Next, you'll need to address the very practical issue of your **financial resources**. If yours is a church-backed project, have you agreed a budget with a line manager? Do you have funding from an external source? Whatever your funding arrangements, make sure that you keep careful track of this side of your project. The key question is – does your budget match your vision? Notice how I've framed that question, by the way – the question isn't whether your vision matches your budget; setting youth ministry vision isn't like buying a car. The vision comes first; *then* you have to work out if and how you're going to make it work financially.

Some things cost more than others, and so, depending on the nature of your dreams, you may need to look at fund-raising. If for instance you want to build a skate ramp in the grounds of your church (don't dismiss it – there may be some visionary minister, somewhere…), you may be looking at raising a significant extra sum; you may alternatively have much less costly ambitions. Either way, you should know exactly how much money you have to spend before you start doing youth work – otherwise you will incur unexpected costs without a certain source from which to fund them.

Alongside this, you should also work out and detail the other **physical resources** that are available to you. Is there a minibus which, if you obtained the relevant qualifications, you might be allowed to borrow? Is there a massive stock of 1970s sports equipment buried at the back of one of the cupboards in your church hall? Is your church connected to a retreat or residential centre somewhere? Again, make a list, in whatever way you find helpful, of all the apparatus and property that might (with permission) be useful in your youth ministry.

A huge question at this point is what kind of potential **venue**(s) you have access to. While this shouldn't necessarily determine the shape of your work (because, let's face it, that's one of the biggest traps that adult church falls into), an assigned meeting place will provide you with a useful base. If your church or project doesn't have its own venue, you need to make a decision: are you going to find a local hall or similar in which to meet (which is likely to require funding), or will your work be entirely based on teenage turf: either in school or in a detached setting (or both)?

Youth work funding
Chris Curtis

There are thousands of grant-making Trusts in the UK, giving anywhere from a few hundred pounds to many millions to different projects and good causes. Can a church access some of these funds for their youth work?

The answer is a qualified "yes". Certainly some churches have had considerable success in doing so, but don't expect it to be an easy process. Finding funding through grants requires a huge amount of research and work and, of course, it may not even pay off with a successful result.

The first challenge is matching a grant-making Trust to your project, or an aspect of your project. Is there a Trust somewhere who will want to fund what you do? How do you start looking? Here are a few options:

• Do the "leg work". Various guides publish lists of Trusts and the kind of work they fund. You can search through these and find those that cover your kind of work. The catch? Apart from the time it takes, many of the directories and databases (and often the most thorough) are subscription based so there's a cost. If you search your networks and contacts, you may be fortunate to find someone who already subscribes to one as part of their job and they may be able to provide information for you free of charge.

- Hire a professional fundraiser. Often the most successful approach, because you are not only hiring their knowledge of trusts but also, in many cases, their personal connections. ("I applied to that Trust last year for another charity and I know the Director... I'll give him a call and talk to him about you and what you're doing..."). Previously many fundraisers worked for commission, taking a percentage of the funds raised. This is much less common today. Expect to pay around £500 a day for the services of an established fundraiser. A funding programme might typically involve two to three days a month for six months... so costs could reach anywhere between £3,600 and £9,000. However, if it results in £100,000 income you may consider it money well spent!

- Use your own contacts. Almost everyone knows someone linked to a grant making trust, but few remember or recognise the link. Interview your church members, leadership team and parents of the young people to see which trusts you might be able to approach using a personal contact.

Once you've found some Trusts to apply to, you'll need to convince them that you have a clear plan for your youth work. At a minimum this means you need to have definite aims and outcomes. So a youth project seeking funding won't get very far with:

> *"We've always had a full time youth worker and they've been really useful in the church. That's why we want to fund another one now."*

But this is better:

> *"We employ a youth worker to provide services to the young people on the housing estate around the church. The aim is to support young people in their emotional, social and spiritual development. We expect to work with 150 young people in depth each year who are facing difficulties in these areas."*

To find funding you'll need to have thought through and written down:

1. What's the aim of the project?

2. What activities will you do to achieve your aim (Trusts tend to call these OUTPUTS).

3. What difference will you make to young people (Trusts tend to call these OUTCOMES).

Spending time thinking through you aims and outcomes will really help when it comes to filling in application forms for Trusts - like many challenges in life, it's about careful planning and lots of hard work. But church youth projects all over the UK successfully secure funds this way every year. With hard work and prayer, you could be one too.

Chris Curtis is the CEO of Youthscape (www.youthscape.co.uk). Follow him on Twitter @chriscurtis.

Models

As I explained at the start of this chapter, there is huge variety in the style and approaches seen in modern youth ministry. In an effort to connect relevantly with the emerging generations, youth workers have often been the pioneering edge of the church, and have seen amazing results in many cases. As you now think about starting something new, or reinvigorating a tired youth ministry, I want to encourage you not to jump straight to the most obvious and tried-and-tested model of a programme-based regular meeting of young people in a room looking at the Bible and various issues. This may well be where you end up, but I would encourage you – now you have done the work of listening to your community, to God, and to your own vision – to consider if what you do might have a slightly – or radically – different shape.

Whatever shape your youth ministry takes, however, I would suggest that it adheres to a few overarching principles:

The message stays the same – This is probably obvious, but it needs saying. In our efforts to connect relevantly with young people, the method we use will constantly change. What doesn't change, however, is the gospel message with which ultimately we're trying to connect them. Man and God were separated because of sin; because of His great love for us, God sent His only Son to die on the cross to open up the way back to Him. His Son, Jesus, was then raised to life, ascended to heaven, and will one day return to usher in a glorious eternity in which we have been offered a place. None of that is negotiable. The way in which we communicate that, however, needs to change; needs to respond (as Paul did on Mars Hill in Acts 17) to the shifting and unstable culture. Trends and technological developments move so fast that the church needs to be on its toes, or see its message get left behind.

In practice, that means understanding how young people receive and participate in stories (see my previous books, *The Ideas Factory* and *The Think Tank,* for much more on this), how they relax and entertain themselves, and the values and priorities of youth culture(s). But, whomever we're speaking to, while the way we share our faith might change, the faith we share shouldn't.

Youth ministry should always be mission-shaped – That is to say, it's never good enough (in my opinion) to build something that simply seeks to grow and nurture young Christians. The door should always be open, in one way or another. The most effective method of youth evangelism bar none is peer to peer: young people reaching their mates, and your youth ministry should seek to enable that. (A fine resource built for exactly this purpose is YFC's *Art of Connecting* course, which helps young people to share the gospel with their friends through the "three story" approach: listen to their story; share your story; connect both to God's big story.)

I'm not being prescriptive here, insisting you should run evangelistic courses or proclamation-based events. Rather, the important point is that we should all take a look at our youth ministry from time to time and examine it through a missional lens: is this a place where unchurched young people would feel comfortable? Is an invitation regularly (or ever) extended for others outside the group to come along? Do the Christian young people pray regularly for their mates?

Belong, behave, believe – There continues to be much debate about the "right" order of these three terms, used to describe the stages a young person moves through when joining a Christian youth group.

This is my order: first, a group should be unreservedly welcoming to young people, treating any behavioural issues with as much outrageous grace as it can muster. Young people are desperate for a space where they belong; we have to give it to them – to love them unconditionally – because that is the church's calling: to love even when it hurts. Once a young person feels settled, loved, and accepted, then you can begin to address behavioural concerns. You should do so gently, patiently, and with compassion, explaining to the young person that their behaviour isn't a barrier to their participation or belonging in the group, but that it does effect their peers' enjoyment of that same experience. Once these two stages have been passed, the young person should be happy, accepted by and comfortable in the group. He or she will naturally build relationships with others in the group, hopefully forming a commitment to it in the longer term.

It is at this point, in my opinion, that the question of faith and belief will naturally be addressed. When a young person has been given a place to belong where they feel safe and accepted, when genuine relationships have been formed not in the interest of obtaining a "conversion" but out of genuine care, then we have earned the right to challenge young people with the message and the offer of Jesus.

With those overarching principles in mind, then, it's time to think about what kind of youth ministry you want to establish. What follows is by no means an exhaustive list of approaches – far from it, and I hope that this book, and the thought and prayer processes that run alongside it, will inspire you to re-imagine Christian youth work completely so that it might be most effective in your context. As a helpful baseline, though, here are some tried-and-tested methods for Christian youth groups. They're not mutually exclusive; some churches would run several of the following approaches.

Church-based youth group

This cannot fail to seem like a caricature, but the majority of Christian youth work looks something like this: young people meet together, once or twice a week, in a church-owned venue such as a hall or lounge. There is an element of socializing (perhaps one of two meetings is based on a programme of activities), and then an element of programmed Christian discipleship activities. There may be some youth-focused worship. The social aspect allows for young people to "belong before they believe", and also creates space for all young people to build relationships both with one another and with their leaders. The faith-focused aspect is one context for youth discipleship (as they learn about, and how to follow, Jesus); participation (they aren't simply an audience; they shape, and can be involved in leading, the group); and evangelism (as young people who have found a sense of belonging begin to believe).

The mix of social and spiritual (although, of course, everything should in some sense be both) is an important balance to get right. There isn't a "magic" percentage split in my experience; some groups will be frustrated by your spending too much time on social activities when they're hungry to meet with God. Others will thrive in the downtime; neither example is wrong.

How this looks in practice will depend somewhat on the resources available to you, and especially on human resources. If you are a volunteer, working with a small team of further volunteers, you may be unable to commit to more than one night's activities a week. If you're employed part-time (or even full-time), or are able to give up more time, you might choose to hold two meetings per week. I have volunteered in youth ministries that have tried both of these approaches (one social meeting and one Bible/programme-based meeting per week, versus an all-in-one meeting with aspects of both); each worked well in its own way. If you do have the resources to provide two different meetings, however, then I'd argue that this is preferable.

Open youth club

A very different approach, and one which is likely to immediately meet very different needs, is a Christian-run open youth club. The budget cuts in the statutory youth sector in recent years mean that fewer such clubs exist for young people now than in the past; yet the rising cost of most entertainment for young people means the need for such clubs is now greater than ever. In a local community youth club, the emphases are on creating a safe space for young people to build positive relationships and spend their free time well. It could be that, in your local area, young people have limited options for how they spend their free time; a drop-in youth club, where a laid-back programme of activities is organized but not enforced on young people, could be an amazing service to those young people.

Such a club will need leisure equipment – a pool table, table football, video games, etc. – housed in a venue that is welcoming and comfortable. This approach may entail more upfront cost to the church; but this is also the kind of project that will be attractive to external funders, such as a local council. Before launching a youth club like this, it would be a good idea to find out who is responsible for youth services in your local council, and to explore the idea for partnership and/or grant funding with them.

Just because you're mainly providing a social and recreational space, however, doesn't mean there's no space for spirituality. A church-run social club should have its colours nailed firmly to the mast – everyone who comes along should be aware that the project is run by Christians. This is so that, when you do decide to talk about faith, no one can complain that they've been misled. You will decide what kind of faith-based content is appropriate, but many such clubs employ the "God slot" – a ten-minute gathering at some point in the evening (usually near the end), during which everyone agrees to listen and be quiet (your part of the bargain being that you'll promise to keep it short). You might use this time to tell a story (similarly to in a school assembly), ask open questions, and provoke thought on issues of spirituality. As you might in school, talk in terms of what you believe, rather than what is true – but don't preach. A club like this is not the place, rather, it's a space for first contact with the sort of young people who usually wouldn't go anywhere near a church or church-run initiative.

Youth congregation

Few youth-ministry models provoke such passionate debate as separate youth church. Advocates say that youth congregations create the sort of relevant worship service that will draw young people in and keep them there; critics call this "ghetto church", and argue that those who grow up in a youth-only church will find it difficult or even impossible to integrate into an all-age church context when they reach adulthood.

I am one of the advocates – I have seen the model work well and, of all the youth ministries I have ever volunteered in, this seems to be the one that has seen the greatest percentage of active faith retention in its "graduates". One of the great joys of my life right now is continuing to bump into former teenage congregants – now in their mid-twenties – and discovering that not only have the majority continued to practise their Christian faith, but several are now working full-time in ministry.

The model that worked for us was a surprisingly similar one to that used by most churches. Sung worship, led by a youth band (itself led by a young adult with a passion for mentoring and bringing on young musicians), a talk given by one of the leaders, or occasionally one of the older teenagers, and a time of praying for the world and each other. That was it. Not, as the idiom goes, rocket science. We had well over 100 young people participating every week, and young people prioritized it in a way that they might not have done a youth "group". Many teenagers became Christians, and the group of young people grew in both depth and number.

But… those young people seldom went into the adult church. The youth congregation was their church, not the meeting that happened to be held in the adjoining hall at the same time. Many church leaders will struggle to see the positives in this model, which effectively means there will be even fewer young faces in their pews on Sunday. Be prepared, then, for a robust discussion with your church leader, if you do decide to explore this route.

Uniformed group

One of the most instantly recognizable forms of youth work, Christian-based uniformed organizations take the activity and achievement-based model of the Scouts and Guides and add a (stronger) faith element. These shouldn't simply be seen as a traditional model – for some young people they are the perfect context for faith development because of their holistic focus. There is great variety within the organizations – some Girls Brigade groups, for example, don't wear a uniform at all; some groups still do a once-a-month "church parade" march. The basic premise, however, is the same: groups of young people (usually all of one gender) meet weekly to have fun and share faith (like most youth groups), with the added dimension of learning skills.

If you're in a place where there are no young people at all, such a group would make a very good starting point. To find out more about what modern uniformed organizations have to offer, contact:

Girls Brigade: 01235 510 425, www.girlsb.org.uk
Boys Brigade: 01442 231 681, www.boys-brigade.org.uk
Campaigners: (England and Wales) 0247 650 5758; (Scotland) 01463 249 900.

Small/cell groups

Again, these may well act as complementary meetings to a main weekly meeting. Small groups of up to ten young people (in my experience, the group dynamics change significantly above that number) meet on a weekly or fortnightly basis to talk about God, faith, and their lives. This is basically the youth version of the adult "house group", but hopefully with less staring at the floor. Generally these take place in homes, so you'll need families who are prepared regularly to host a group of young people; alternatively, you might meet in different areas of a church or other building if you have access.

The massive *advantage* of such groups is that, generally speaking, they are where memorable and lasting discipleship can happen. Not exclusively, of course – some teenagers have life-changing experiences in a tent full of 10,000 people – but this kind of atmosphere – a group of friends who like and trust each other, sharing honestly and deeply together – is highly conducive to "sticky" faith.

The big *challenge* is safety. Best practice is always to have more than one adult leading a group, so if these groups are going to have adult involvement, you are potentially going to need a lot of DBS-checked volunteers; more if the groups grow and multiply. One possible solution to this is to have the host parent agree to be present (on the same floor of the house, with the door open) during the meeting, but this asks a lot of them.

Small groups don't have to be led by adults, however – and preferably, in the long term, yours won't be. If you are able to develop some young leaders within your youth ministry, then leading their peers is a great safe place for them to grow and develop those skills. The long-term goal, then, could be to have a number of midweek small groups, which young people choose to attend in addition to their main youth-group meeting(s) and/or church, led by young people. They should have three growth aims – for young people to grow in their faith, grow their commitment to one another in community and, through inviting their friends along, grow in number.

If all this sounds a bit daunting, and a world away from your limited resources and numbers, don't worry. This is also a great way to launch a new youth group: meeting in a relaxed home setting, sharing life, opening the Bible together. Small groups prove that big isn't always beautiful; deeper questions, quiet reflection, and real honesty are all facilitated by low-number, high-trust meetings like this.

School-based

Every youth worker should try to find a way of engaging with local schools. Aside from being the place where young people spend a huge part of their lives, they are also the one place where all the young people in your community gather. If at all possible, this should be a part of your overall approach to youth ministry (see Amy Stock's mini-article for a quick how-to), but it may be that you want to go further.

A youth ministry might be entirely focused on – or even based in and around – local schools. Faith schools are a particularly good place to start, but others might be equally open to your help – if that really is what you're offering. No school wants Christians who are simply going to come in and proselytize, but if you're prepared to offer genuine services – teaching balanced lessons, taking assemblies, or being available as a chaplain or mentor – then they may well be interested. The Anglican Diocese of Blackburn has been involved in some particularly innovative work in this area – placing Diocesan Youth Officers (youth workers/co-ordinators employed by the diocese itself) within schools. Some particularly good examples of schools-based work are listed below; if this is an area that interests you, check out some of the diocesan websites, or make contact with the one nearest to you.

Diocese of Blackburn (http://www.bdeducation.org.uk/parish-based-training.html)
East to West (www.easttowest.org.uk/)
LCET (http://www.lcet.org/)
Leeds Faith In Schools (http://www.lfis.org/)
LiNX (http://www.linxyouth.net)
Sparkfish (http://www.sparkfish.org.uk/)

Schools work from scratch

Amy Stock

Imagine being part of a staff team in which teachers and support staff come to you to talk about what is really important in their lives; imagine students who respect your Christian faith and ask you questions about why it is so important to you; imagine broken and hurting young people whose lives get turned around because they finally have someone to sit with them and allow them to process life; imagine being able to make an impact in a school environment by just being yourself and letting God work through you.

OK, so that's the dream, but where do you start? Here are five things to think about before approaching your local school:

1. Ask yourself what you want to achieve by visiting a school. You need to be clear about why you want to work in the school and be able to communicate the same message about that at the front of your church as you do in the head teacher's office on a Monday morning. Be as specific as you can; yes, you want to share God's love, but what does that look like?

2. Do some research about what the schools are like in your area. Some background knowledge and an idea of challenges and opportunities available in your local schools is essential. For example, are there any schools in special measures or are there any specialist colleges focusing on areas that are strengths of yours (very often schools with have a specialism, e.g. Arts or Technology). Are there academies that have flexibility when it comes to religious education? You have something valuable to offer when it comes to spiritual input, so do not be put off if RE is not even on the curriculum of the academy; there are all sorts of creative ways that you can invest in this environment.

3. What age group do you want to work with? Just because you work with teenagers at the weekend does not limit you to working in secondary schools. Consider how working in primary schools and particularly with ten- and eleven-year-olds could affect your youth-work strategy. At the same time, find out what colleges or sixth forms there are in your area. This is a key time for Christian young people to start emerging as young leaders and also an age when important life choices are made. Your presence in their sixteen–nineteens education could make all the difference in their lives.

4. Be realistic about how much time you have to give. Unless you are doing something very wrong, a school would be crazy to not bite your hand off for extra support, so decide before you approach them how much time you can spare. Be clear about this and let schools know your remit for visiting them and what they can expect from you. It is far better to promise less and over-deliver than to over-promise and let them down later on. Good schools work is based on reliability, trust, and strong relationships.

5. Do you have any connections with staff or school governors? If you know of no one at your church, ask around and visit other churches to find links with the school; I guarantee that you will find some. Meet them for coffee, chat about the culture of the school, and paint them a picture of how you might like to get involved. Then listen and take their advice. They can help you to think through what skills you have to offer and to consider whether you need to look for training in new areas.

Arranging that first appointment in the school could be the best decision you ever make, so do not be afraid of it. Most of the children and young people in your area will never set foot inside a church building. Will you accept the challenge to take church to them?

Amy Stock is the Director of Schoolswork.co.uk. Follow her on Twitter @amystock

Detached work

One of the key motivations for doing work in schools is that you are leaving the relative safety of the church and going to where young people are, rather than waiting for them to come and find you. A similar rationale underpins detached youth work – the "detached" referring to the fact that it takes place on young people's own "turf", and may well never actually move into the church. This could be a big deal for some church leaders, if in their minds the main reason for your work is eventually to increase the numbers of young people engaged and involved with their church. If, however, your vision – and theirs – is to see young people in your community moved by the love of God, and the kingdom extended even if the size of the church isn't, then spending part or even all of your youth-ministry time in detached work could be a viable and even a prophetic move.

Don't simply walk up to a group of unknown teenagers in the park. Get some advice from one of the brilliant Christian charities that specialize in this area. The Frontier Youth Trust (FYT) is a fantastic organization full of visionary people, and it has been around for a good while. The StreetSpace initiative, which is affiliated to FYT, is a practical and fairly low-cost way to get a detached Christian youth-work project started – in return for a time commitment (and a reasonable fee), StreetSpace will train and support you in starting and sustaining a detached work in your area. The organization's non-linear model aims to take young people on a journey from cold contact to some expression of community or church.

Frontier Youth Trust: www.fyt.org.uk

StreetSpace: www.streetspace.org.uk

Detached Youth Work
John Wheatley

Some youth workers meet young people in youth clubs, some in cafés, and some in schools... And some youth workers leave the confines of their buildings and venture onto the streets to meet young people – that is Detached Youth Work.

> *Friday night, summer, we are walking around our local park and we meet a group of lads playing football. Two are sitting on the edge watching, drinking Red Bull and smoking. "Hey, how's it going? Can we join you?" We sit with them for half an hour; we talk about the school holidays, the football, where they got their cigarettes from.*

Detached Youth Work is an extremely relational approach to youth work. No buildings, no venues, just the streets and parks. It intends to reach young people who would never normally go into a youth venue, let alone a church.

It might be helpful to first define two other similar but different methods of youth work: Mobile and Outreach.

Mobile Youth Work – taking a "venue" like an activity bus or portable skate ramps to where the young people are (i.e. the park);

Outreach Work – going out to find young people in order to invite them back to an activity or club (either now or in the future).

Neither of these is Detached Youth Work because of the power dynamics. Detached Youth Work uses the street, park, graveyard, or bus stop as the "venue" for youth work – this rebalances power in favour of the young people and puts youth work in their context.

So why do it? For a start there are no heating, equipment, or rent costs; there is no need for a massive team to staff a venue, just two volunteers will do; and there is no need to enforce difficult ground rules. The street is a neutral setting, one that the young people who spend time there call their own. Instead of asking them into your venue with your rules, Detached Youth Workers enter the space of the young people.

It's like a missionary venture. We are familiar with the idea of missionaries going overseas into a different culture, learning new ways of living, and sharing the good news of the gospel in a fresh and meaningful way. When meeting young people beyond the walls of the church the same process is needed – young people live in a different culture.

Detached Youth Workers must enter the world of the young people, learn their ways, build strong relationships, and tell the gospel afresh in their culture. Detached Youth Work intentionally reaches young people who would otherwise have no opportunity of hearing about the Christian story. These young people need courageous adults who will cross the gulf of culture to get to know them, growing with them a church relevant to the context.

Detached Youth Work is an exciting opportunity – and the street can be an exhilarating place to be in the evening. But doing it right requires a little bit of knowledge, a good framework, and a lot of common sense. So here are my top tips:

Never work alone – Get a team of at least two, along with an emergency contact.

Know what you are getting into – Research the area, know what to do in an emergency, and think through some of the ethical questions you might face on the street (i.e. will you sit with a group of young people while they smoke?).

Find a good framework/oversight structure – Perhaps read *Meet Them Where They're At* (available on Kindle) or join StreetSpace (a community of Christian detached youth workers).

Let other people know what you are doing – It will help you if you are supported by your church and local community. Contact the police and local services. Get the word out there.

See it through to the end – Detached Youth Work is a relational way of working, and relationships need time. Commit to long-term regular work for the best impact.

John Wheatley is a youth worker with StreetSpace, an initiative of Frontier Youth Trust, and a community of missional youth workers working in some of the UK's toughest contexts. Visit: www.streetspace.org.uk

What is success?

I hope this list has helped you to think a bit more about the kind of youth-ministry project that you could start in your community.

Before we move on, there's just one more question to ask yourself, and it lays the groundwork for evaluation later. What does success look like for you and your team? At the start of this chapter, we looked at outcomes – what you hope to achieve – and so, as we return to this theme, let's think about the even bigger picture.

Thinking over three, five, and even ten years, how might your community change as a result of what you're going to do? Don't believe that this kind of thinking is pie in the sky; just watch one of those glitzy TV awards shows that reward and recognize local volunteers, and you'll see plenty of stories of communities that have been hugely influenced by the lifelong commitment of one or two heroic people: the man who has coached the same boys' football team in a poverty-stricken town for forty years; the Brownie pack leader who has helped and encouraged over 1,000 girls.

If you invest with vision for the long term, you can see whole areas affected for good, and even changed. So take some time in prayer to listen again to God; meditate on the size and complexity of God's story as revealed through the Bible, and reflect on how, in God's economy, really good things can take time.

Further reading

Meet Them Where They're At (new Kindle edition) – Richard Passmore, Porthouse, 2011
Schools Ministry as Mission – Nick Shepherd, Y12 e-book, Grove, 2008
Stories from the Edge – Dave Wiles, Monarch, 2010
Youth Ministry: A Multifaceted Approach – Ed. Sally Nash, SPCK, 2011

5

Practice and Programme

So by now, all being well, you've worked out what your youth ministry is going to look like.

Now, what on earth are you going to do with the young people when they start to turn up? By this point, the readers of this book are hopefully falling into various diverse categories – from full-time youth ministers relaunching a city youth café, to absolute beginners starting a new Bible study group, and everything in between.

This presents something of a problem as we come to look at programmes, since your style and content will vary dramatically depending on your chosen model. What I'll attempt to do in this chapter is to lay out some building blocks which are applicable to the practice of any expression of youth ministry, and then move on to suggest a few potential starting points for developing a programme.

Building block 1: The Bible

It doesn't matter what kind of youth ministry you're involved in. Even if the vast majority of the work doesn't involve any formal "spiritual" content, the Bible underpins and shapes our work with young people – and if it doesn't, that's the equivalent of going orienteering without a map or a compass: you're just going to be wandering around aimlessly.

What does that mean in practice? Firstly, it means that you, the youth leader, should be grounded and regularly immersed in the word of God for your own benefit – to the extent that the Bible shapes and informs your world view and, in turn, the way you lead, speak, and respond to others. If you're going to minister in a Christlike way – taking on some of Jesus' character and following His example – then you will naturally need to be familiar with His words and story. If you're going to be equipped to answer difficult and searching questions, you will need to continually return to the word of God in your own life and study.

Secondly, then – and linked to the above – you should allow the Bible to shape your practice. Read Paul, and the adventures of the early church. Read the Gospels over again. What is God saying to you, through the stories of New Testament mission, about the way in which you could or should address the holistic needs of your community? As you begin to think about a programme, commit to prayerfully reading these stories, and others. Ask God, as a leadership team – which passages of Scripture are particularly important and relevant to your particular work. If you come up with some answers to this, write those verses down, and refer to them regularly.

The Bible should also be a practical and present feature of your youth work. If you're running an open youth club, that might mean carrying a Bible around in your pocket (possibly loaded onto a mobile device), therefore being equipped and prepared to bring it out when conversation demands it. If you're running a group that includes a time-limited amount of spiritual input (such as a God slot within a mainly social group or club), then make sure that input has the richness and the quality that comes from sharing and imparting biblical truth. Don't stop at "spiritual" stories – expose young people to the living, thrilling, fascinating word of God. And if you're running a group that might include a considerable amount of faith input, again I urge you to put the Bible at the heart of your programme.

I say all this (when perhaps it could be taken as read) because I fear that, sometimes, we can become a little embarrassed about sharing Scripture with young people. We talk around themes (which are important and relevant, and get teenagers talking about real life), but sometimes we can struggle to connect them effectively with Scripture. We might find a few "proof texts" to demonstrate that God is interested in something, but we worry that reading a whole passage or chapter might switch young people off. We needn't worry. As Charles Spurgeon reportedly once said: "Defend the Bible? I would as soon defend a lion! Unchain it, and it will defend itself."

Sharing the Bible
Mark Walley

Picture the scene: you've started up your new youth club and you've got four or five guys down on the first night. You've played some icebreakers, including the really messy one involving spaghetti, and you've all drunk far too much coke. Your assistant leader has just led them through a game of dodgeball without anyone killing each other or the church building suffering any damage you can't cover up. And now you turn to them and say, "Alright, guys, let's gather round; we're going to get out some Bibles and hear about Jesus." How do you feel? Does your stomach drop slightly as you wonder how you're going to persuade people that reading this book is worthwhile? Do you hope everyone will be quiet so it's over quickly? Is the temptation to basically skip over the Bible to get to what you want to say, which will be more interesting than what God has to say about Himself?

The Bible is the word of God, written for us by human authors under the inspiration of the Holy Spirit. In the words of 2 Timothy 3:16 it's "God-breathed". God still uses it to speak to people through His Spirit, revealing to them His Son Jesus. That's phenomenally profound. The God of the heavens and earth will use His Bible to speak to us people on earth. More specifically, when people read the Bible trusting in Him, He sends His Spirit to open up their ears and eyes to learn about His Son Jesus, so people might look upon Him and trust in all He's done.

So here's the thing: often when we gloss over or are scared of using the Bible with young people we're saying at least one of two things. We're saying we don't think God will speak through the Bible to them today, and we're saying we don't think young people will understand what's spoken. We need to realize these two beliefs are lies. God promises to speak to people today through His word. He promises to show people Jesus through the words. And because understanding God's word depends on God's Spirit revealing it to them, young people can understand in the same way as everyone else.

Will young people (especially non-Christians) really want to read the Bible, though? Well, from experience, yes. Currently we run four Bible studies for a range of young people who are from Christian and non-Christian backgrounds. But they don't work if you trick people into them: don't lure people in with games and fun and then spring a Bible study on them. Instead, invite young people to come along and read the Bible (and play some games or whatever); you'll be amazed by their response. When it comes to teaching them, remember that the Holy Spirit is the one doing the work; at the simplest and profoundest level, all you need to do is pray, open up the Bible, and tell the young people to look at and hear about Jesus in the passage.

Mark Walley is the Youth Worker at All Souls Club House, London. Follow him on Twitter @sparticus

Building block 2: Voluntary Participation

Danny Brierley, in his 2002 *Youthwork* magazine series which later formed the basis of his book *Going Deeper* (Authentic, 2003), identifies four key values of youth work and ministry which form the basis of the next three "building blocks". Each is drawn from the values behind secular or "statutory" youth work, but, given a spiritual twist, each applies to youth ministry.

The first of these values, Voluntary Participation, is hugely important – it's what separates youth work from school teaching. The distinctive element in youth work is that its participants make an active choice to be present and take part. School attendance is compulsory by law; coming along to a church-based youth group is a matter of free choice. In some cases, young people are pressurized into attending church-related activities... this isn't voluntary participation. Similarly, if we hide our intentions – inviting them to attend an open youth club, but either not making clear that it is run by a Christian group, or surprising them with spiritual content – this isn't voluntary participation either.

Rather, our aim should be to present young people with an open-handed offer of provision for them, and an opportunity to reject it. That might sound naïve, but think about it. If young people don't really want to be there, can we really expect them to develop an interest in the faith we're promoting? If we try to trick young people into encountering Christianity, do we really expect God to use such duplicity? The challenge for youth workers is to make engagement in their activities both entirely voluntary and entirely compelling. In this case, whoever chooses to attend has already made a step on the journey simply by being present.

The second half of this expression, Participation, is also important. Youth ministry (and church, for that matter) shouldn't be about creating a passive audience of consumers to whom we bring faith, hope, and love. Instead, we should be encouraging teenagers to be active participants in whatever group or activity we involve them in.

What this means in practice will vary according to your youth-work model. If you're running a youth congregation, then rather than creating compelling services with your superbly able team of adult volunteers and wowing your audience of teenagers with a weekly event that is almost as slick as a big-tent summer event, you should act counter-intuitively. Get the young people's ideas, and use them. Draw together a youth band and persist with them, even if they struggle at first. Mentor and develop those with communications gifts, and allow them to share a talk. Doing this may be far less professional, but the participants will learn and grow far more. They will have opportunities through this to develop their gifts, but even more importantly they'll see they have a role to play in church now, rather than having to wait until they're "old enough".

If you're running an open youth club, this might mean forming a committee of some of the more active participants and giving them a genuine say in the running of the club, especially the programme. Again, handing over ownership in this way will give the young people opportunities to use and develop skills, to demonstrate commitment to the group, and to invite their friends. Whatever your programme and model look like, make sure they are set up for participants, not customers.

This kind of thinking touches on another of Brierley's key values, Empowerment. Our young people are now growing up in a culture that is subtly devaluing and disempowering them. As we've seen in previous chapters, the right-wing media is particularly scathing about teenagers and their potential. Young people are stigmatized as "hoodies", "NEETs",[5] "chavs", and "yobs". An extension of participation, empowerment sees us giving back value and power to a generation for whom these things have been eroded. That's why inviting a young person to join an organizing committee, or a youth band, or giving them a position of responsibility, is so powerful and important. In an increasingly paedophobic culture, such actions are positively prophetic.

Building block 3: Informal education

Youth ministry isn't about entertainment. That's not to say that the activities of Christian youth work shouldn't be fun, but that isn't an end in itself. Youth ministry is about development; helping young people to grow as individuals, in community, and in faith. Informal education – creating opportunities for young people to learn and

---

5   An acronym for "Not in Education, Employment or Training".

develop through non-formal methods in non-formal contexts – is another important component underpinning strong, potentially-transformational youth ministry.

Since the 1970s, the notion of relational youth ministry has become steadily more influential. This is the idea that, as youth workers, we lead and disciple young people by getting among them, building appropriate friendships, and "doing life" with them. Through building strong relationships with young people, youth workers are able to understand what is really going on in their world, to model to them close-up what being a Christian looks like, and to engage them in deep and far-reaching conversation.

The content of that conversation should on one level be relaxed, informal, and driven by the young person, but on another level there is intentionality on the part of the youth worker to explore the area of faith in God. We "earn the right" to talk to young people about Jesus, although we should be at least equally motivated by genuine care and compassion for them as children of God.

In youth ministry, then, we should seek to inspire, provoke, and challenge young people to learn and make decisions about God. We should seek also to give them opportunities to learn more about who they are; to develop and practise skills; to grow in their own relational awareness and ability. Our programmes should reflect this.

Building block 4: Equality of opportunity

In youth ministry, we are determined not to repeat the mistakes of previous generations, and in young people we find a group who have no intention of doing so. In the twenty-first century we are beginning to emerge from centuries and centuries of unfair cultural prejudice on the basis of gender, sexuality, colour, race, creed, or physical ability. We certainly enjoy a more enlightened society than those that preceded us, yet the job is far from done. Our sinful nature means that we are still conditioned to make negative judgments against people who are different from us (read Malcolm Gladwell's fascinating book *Blink* for some particularly damning insights into this).[6]

Equality of opportunity is not simply an important and worthy value for youth ministry, then, it is also one about which we must be intentional. In our informal education context, young people will learn subtle lessons about how to treat those who look different from us from the way we act as leaders in this regard. It is crucially important that we treat everyone with equal dignity and respect and – this is vital – that we give every young person a fair and equal chance.

Equality of opportunity isn't only about avoiding negative prejudice, however; it's about proactively ensuring that every young person gets just as much chance to shine, learn, participate, and grow as the next. Again, this sounds perfectly easy to agree to – but in practice it becomes more difficult. If you're running a table-tennis tournament, it's easy enough to ensure that everyone gets an equal chance to compete (although some will, like me, have all the ping-pong ability of a dead newt). If you're putting on a youth church service, however, true equality of opportunity requires a big commitment. Do the good-looking, talented, eloquent kids get to stand on the stage and lead, while their quieter, less forthright friends get to look after the tea urn or hand out service sheets? Aiming for equality not of ability – since that isn't in our hands – but of opportunity, is a sometimes-difficult but vitally important process for youth workers. We serve a God who sees "neither Jew nor Greek, slave nor free, male nor female... for you are all one in Christ Jesus" (Galatians 3:28). Our youth-ministry approach should reflect the same heart – seeing each person as both unique and equal.

My wife and I were "church-shopping" (a horrifically consumerist phrase, but you get the idea) after we were married, and

---

6   Malcolm Gladwell, *Blink: The Power of Thinking Without Thinking*, Penguin, 2006.

had struggled to find a place that felt like home. One week, we found ourselves sitting at the back of an open evangelical church with a small but committed congregation, and after several weeks of Bono-style failure to find what we were looking for, our hopes weren't high. Then, before the sermon, a young man took to the stage to deliver the reading. It was clear, after all of a second, that this man had both mental and physical health problems, and reading did not come easily to him. For a moment I felt uncomfortable, but then, as I realized that the rest of the room was quite relaxed, I simply sat back and listened. It wasn't easy for him, but he got the whole reading out, audibly and coherently. We'd all heard every word and, what's more, those words were speaking powerfully. Now the minister of that church – which we immediately decided to join – had not taken the easy route when selecting his reader for that morning. He knew that to invest in this man was not as straightforward as, say, asking the trained actress in the congregation to read instead. But as he had extended an opportunity to this man, who surely spent his life being overlooked by others, he had facilitated a quite prophetic moment. As we work with young people of all backgrounds and abilities, we should look to do the same.

Youth work and gender
Jenny Baker

People have been debating for centuries about whether our gender – what we understand masculinity and femininity to be and how we practise it – is down to nature or nurture. That debate will continue, but there's no doubt that some aspects of gender are constructed by the environment in which we're brought up and our early interactions with other people. Studies have shown that girls and boys are treated differently from birth, even by parents who think they are being neutral in their parenting. Girls learn that they get affirmed for what they look like, and that they're expected to be compliant and passive and to take care of others; boys learn that they get approval when they are physical, but that playing with dolls gets them strange looks, and that "big boys don't cry". It's a complex process but an accumulation of these types of interaction creates an expectation of what's normal for a boy or a girl, and a restricted set of activities, clothes, behaviours, and ways of expressing themselves that are considered acceptable for each sex.

Youth workers can construct gender too. A female youth worker runs an open youth club on a Friday night where the girls sit and paint each other's nails while the boys play football, dominating most of the space and making lots of noise. There's no overlap between the two activities and no discussion about why the girls don't play football, why boys don't paint their nails, or why sex is an organizing category. By endorsing that divide, the youth worker is communicating something about masculinity and femininity; she's helping to construct gender.

Youth work needs to value young people in all their diversity. If we are to help young people reach their full potential, then we shouldn't have gender-bound restrictions on what that potential might be. What if you have the next female prime minister in your youth group and your girls' work consists of cake baking and manicures and she's not given the opportunity to speak or to see women leading? She'll go elsewhere to develop those skills and find those role models. I wonder how many opportunities we miss to liberate and empower young people into all God is calling them to be, because we don't critique or question the gendered boundaries that are imposed on their lives, or, worse still, because we're enforcing those boundaries ourselves.

So how do you create an environment that enables teenagers to explore their full potential as young women and men?

Use their interests as a starting point but not necessarily an end

Good youth work starts with young people's interests. Some girls love "pampering" activities, such as hand massages. But make sure that providing those activities doesn't communicate that that's what being a girl is all about, or only about. Use that context to critique our culture's emphasis on worth being found in appearance, and help girls base their self-esteem on something much more solid. Projects for boys that offer mainly conventional "male" activities such as sport can build group solidarity, but can also feed into and entrench a very narrow understanding of masculinity – that "real" boys are hard and play football. Youth workers need to think creatively about how they work with boys so that they're able to provide alternatives to that narrow view.

Provide a range of activities

By encouraging young people to try things they've never done before, we can honour and develop the diversity of young people's interests and gifts. We can help them to be more accepting of difference, and introduce them to new things they might grow to love and excel at. Over a number of sessions, make sure there are opportunities for both boys and girls to do activities that are loud, messy, physically demanding, arty, practical, quiet, and thoughtful, that involve talking, that involve making, and so on.

Expand young people's aspirations through what you model

Role models are really important. Think about the stories you tell in talks or as discussion starters; talk about sportswomen as well as sportsmen, for example. Think about the roles that men and women play in the film clips you show and help young people to critique them. Think about the models of work, parenting, leadership, and relationships that your youth team provide. Challenge each other to go beyond stereotypical roles and try new things.

Jenny Baker works for Church Urban Fund and is a co-founder of the Sophia Network for women in leadership: www.sophianetwork.org.uk

What are you going to do now?

Having put those four building blocks in place, we have a sturdy basis for any programme of meetings or activities. If you can agree that your youth work will be fundamentally rooted in the Bible – and therefore in the communication of the love of God through Jesus; in principles of free choice, empowerment, equal opportunity, and a recognition that it is about more than just having fun… then I believe you're in a great position to start developing that programme.

You could skip what I'm about to say, and leap straight to some of the ready-made models below. I'd rather you didn't, though. This might sound strange coming from the long-term editor of a resourcing publication, and the author of several "off-the-shelf" resource books, but my dream is that the church could be full of visionary cultural-contextualizers who at worst seriously adapt ready-to-use resource materials, and at best create their own, perfectly-tailored curricula. I appreciate that in many contexts, especially where resources are sparse, that might sound like a naïve suggestion, and pragmatically I can see that few of us are in a position to do it. But if that's the absolute ideal, then perhaps we can all commit to trying never to deliver pre-written resource material straight "off the shelf". The reason for this, of course, is that just as every young person is a uniquely different child of God, each local context, each community, and each church around the world is subtly (or markedly) different from the next. As we develop programmes that will inspire young people to develop and grow in a relationship with God, then, our planning should take the uniqueness of the local context (and even the young people we are likely to meet) into consideration.

So, as you think about developing a first term's programme, make a fun evening out of it. Draw together your volunteer team (even if that just makes two of you), and if neither of you finds this sort of thing easy, invite one or two friends who understand what you're trying to do and can give helpful input. Talk again about those Big Picture aims that we looked at in the previous chapter; consider and pray through what you want to achieve, and then start planning the most engaging and relevant term you can imagine!

Building on some of the overarching principles of ministry to young people (consistency of message; mission-shaped models; belonging before belief) discussed in chapter four, and the "building blocks" of youth work discussed above, you should be able to develop a programme that, whatever your model, includes:

• Content that helps young people to learn about, and journey towards some decisions on God, Jesus, and the Bible

- Opportunities for young people to relax, build community, belong, and feel empowered
- Elements that enable young people to invite their mates along, regardless of whether they have a faith.

If you can do this, you'll be on your way to addressing both your local need for youth provision and the decline in church engagement among young people. Sound like fun? Then let's proceed.

Whatever you do, start social

Whether you're running the most relaxed club or the most intense Bible study group, I'd suggest you start every year – and perhaps every term – with a purely social gathering. There are plenty of weeks in a term to lead young people on a journey of deep discipleship; it's important that they know, like, and begin to interact with each other first. You can get really creative with this, from hosting a "themed" evening (such as French/Spanish/Mexican night, where you prepare food, music, clothing, and games from a chosen country) to a journey-based activity like a chip review (where you walk around between the various chip-selling emporia of your local area and decide on the best) or progressive supper (three-course meal prepared at three local houses; the group walks between). There are a million different things you could do as an opening-week social activity, so spend a bit of time brainstorming until you come up with something that will excite both leaders and young people.

First programme ideas...

What follows, then, are some suggestions for ten weeks of faith-based content for three generalized contexts. Use them as a starting point for your planning – please don't see them as a finished guide. In each case I've given a subject title, Bible reference (where relevant), and very brief explanation of the idea. You could then address this in all sorts of ways, from bringing in visiting speakers to hosting the session in a different venue from normal. Do not expect any of these guides to provide a comprehensive introduction to the Christian faith, a full overview of the Bible, or a complete guide to apologetics – these are suggestions for one good and potentially first term with a new or revitalized youth group.

...for a series of "God slots" or short opportunities to share a message of faith

Week 1: You matter to God (Psalm 139) – Helping young people to understand their uniqueness in God's eyes; He knows them intimately.

Week 2: You *really* matter to God (John 3:16) – Introducing the big, central concept of Christianity (because, frankly, why would you wait?): God loves each of us so much, He sent His only Son to die in order that we could know Him.

Week 3: Faith story 1 – A leader gives an honest, warts-and-all account of their faith journey, including what made the difference when they decided to follow God, and why they continue to do so now.

Week 4: The God in front of our faces (Romans 1:20) – Putting across Paul's argument that the beauty and diversity of creation clearly point to a creator; and explaining how sometimes we can miss something obvious when it's right in front of our faces.

Week 5: God listens (Matthew 7:7) – God invites us to talk to Him, and to ask Him for help. What might happen if we took Him up on the offer?

Week 6: Faith story 2 – Another leader, helper or visitor shares their story of finding and wrestling with faith.

Week 7: God of miracles (John 2:1–11) – Jesus performed miraculous acts which had a deep impact on the people around Him and have been remembered for millennia. How was He able to do them? Because he was God.

Week 8: God of miracles *today*? (John 14:12) – Jesus told His disciples that, after His death, they'd do even greater things than He did! So can people be healed, or see other miracles happen, today?

Week 9: Faith story 3 – A third leader, helper or visitor gives an honest insight into why they're a Christian.

Week 10: Mark Challenge (Mark 1) – As you break at the end of the term, challenge any in the group who are intrigued by the person and story of Jesus to join you in reading the book of Mark during the break.

...for a group of young people interested in exploring faith

This isn't a ten-week course at the end of which the entire group will be queuing up to give their lives to God (although Youth Alpha [http://run.alpha.org/youth/home] and Christianity Explored Youth [www.ceministries.org/ce/cy] are both excellent resources that aim for exactly that). Again, this is a starting point for a new group.

Week 1: If it's true… Spend a session talking through the implications for all of our lives if there really is a God; if He really does want to know us; if there's a heaven and a hell, and a choice to be made between the two.

Week 2: Who was Jesus 1 (Mark 8) – In the Gospel of Mark, Jesus asks Peter the key question, "Who do you say I am?" This session looks at the key moments in Jesus' life and ministry on earth before posing the question, "So if He wasn't really God, who was He?"

Week 3: Who was Jesus 2 – Using C.S. Lewis' "Mad, Bad or God/ Lunatic, Liar or Lord" argument (find this in *Mere Christianity*),[7] this session picks up from the previous one by exploring possible explanations for who Jesus, this historically recognized person, really was.

Week 4: Why I am a Christian – Either the leader or a relevant invited guest (with whom the young people will find some kind of connection) shares their faith journey and invites questions.

Week 5: Why suffering? (Genesis 3 / Romans 8:18–30) – Four weeks of apologetics begin with the Big One – how can a loving God allow His creations to suffer? This session needs to address the concept and problem of sin, and the idea that natural disasters are part of a deteriorating earth, which also links to the fall.

Week 6: Doesn't the Bible contradict itself? (Isaiah 9:6–7) – This session explores how Jesus perfectly fulfils hundreds of Old Testament prophecies through His life and ministry, and that, while on the surface some individual verses seem to disagree, the Bible is a living word, not an off-the-shelf rulebook, and its meaning is complicated. Many, many people throughout history have dedicated their lives to digging for its hidden treasures, and this is possible because it is so brilliantly complex, and yet also so accessible.

Week 7: How can a loving God send people to hell? (Revelation 20:11–15) – Depending on your theology, you may address this

---

7   C.S. Lewis, *Mere Christianity*, Collins, 2012.

topic differently, but this session will restate the offer of eternal life with God, and the reality that we are free to choose an eternal life without Him. You will explain that God is both perfectly loving and perfectly just; whatever happens to us when we die will be judged through those two lenses.

Week 8: Hasn't science disproved God? – Consider bringing in a Christian who is also a professional scientist, or using clips from the brilliant resource "Test of Faith" (www.testoffaith.com) as you explore how scientific and theological world views are actually compatible, and even help to explain each other.

Week 9: Grill-a-Christian – An ask-anything session where the leader(s) and others agree to answer any question on life and faith. If your church leader agrees, it would be great if he/she was prepared to be one of the panellists in the firing line.

Week 10: If you could pray for one thing (Matthew 7) – Using Jesus' promises about prayer as a stimulus, hold a hypothetical prayer meeting. If there really was a God who could answer prayers, what would the members of your group ask Him for? Then, if they are happy, pray through each of these requests with them.

...for a group of "churched" young people

Of course this category is clumsy, and could describe all sorts of groups. This is a potential programme outline for a mixed group of young people who profess some kind of faith, assuming that some will be fired-up passionate potential group leaders, and others will still be riding on the back of their parents' faith.

Week 1: My story – Ask members of the group to share their life story – and faith journey where applicable. Not everyone has to take part if they don't want to – but if they're happy to share, invite the group to ask them supplementary questions. Make sure one of the leaders goes first in order to calm nerves and set a template. This could take more than one week if it goes well.

Week 2: What is the Christian message? (John 3) – Ask the group to articulate the core of the Christian story, and then use Scripture to address or fill in the gaps. The main points: God is love; Jesus was the Son of God; the cross opens up the way between man and God; we can now choose to follow Jesus.

Week 3: Time with God – How do we cultivate a relationship with God? Through spending time with Him. This session looks at some of the ways in which we can connect with God – especially when we're on our own – and explores how we can fit these rhythms into our everyday life.

Week 4: Blessed are those… 1 (Matthew 5 – 7) – This session looks at Jesus' value system for us and the world, as taught in His "Sermon on the Mount". What did He say, and how does it apply to the way we should live our lives today? Leave the prayer passages out, as these are covered later in the term.

Week 5: Blessed are those… 2 (Matthew 5 – 7) – Continuing to look at Jesus' "Sermon on the Mount" principles. By the end of these two sessions, the young people should have a good grasp of what He said, why, and how it applies to our lives now. Leave the prayer passages out, as these are covered later in the term.

Week 6: Sharing faith 1 (Matthew 28) – This session looks at what Jesus said in His "Great Commission", and explores why He said it. Why is it important that we reach our mates, and what are some practical ways in which we can do it?

Week 7: Sharing faith 2 – Following on, this session will help the young people to think through some of the common barriers they face to sharing faith with their friends, and move on to discuss some of the common objections that their friends might have to Christianity. While not providing straightforward answers, this session should equip the young people with a way of moving the conversation on when they hit a big objection from their non-Christian friend.

Week 8: Prayer power 1 (Matthew 6:5–15) – How did Jesus teach us to pray? We're overfamiliar with the Lord's Prayer, so in this session break it down line by line and look at what God's priorities for prayer seem to be.

Week 9: Prayer power 2 (Matthew 7:7–12) – Jesus offers us answered prayer – how seriously do we take these words? In this session, explore creative ways of praying (perhaps setting up several "prayer stations" and allowing the young people to move between them), and pray some big heartfelt prayers together.

Week 10: Recap week – What has been covered this term, and how does it fit together? (Don't get too disappointed if they can't immediately remember.) Using a worksheet or other prompt, explain how reaching our mates is a big focus for us as a group, and how it's important that we have a good grasp of the Christian story ourselves before we try to explain it to others. Unpack how having a "devotional" life and committing ourselves in prayer are the keys not only to our own healthy walk with God, but to successfully reaching our friends for Him.

Format

Those are just some basic ideas for how a sample term's programme *might* look – but how you deliver this will be dependent on a range of variables beyond their level of faith commitment. For instance, the format you choose for leading a session with a group of eleven-year-old boys (generally speaking high-energy, short punchy shots of information and exciting ideas; lots of opportunity to get practical), will be very different from a session for sixth-formers (much more discussion; fewer silly games; involving them in leading the session). Very generally speaking, a session could include some or all of the following elements:

Introduction: A few words to explain the point and content of the session. For some young people, it's really important to understand why you're addressing a topic; for others, knowing what to expect will relax them.

Icebreaker: A short game designed to bring energy into a room and get people talking. This may or may not bear some relation to the theme of the session. For a brilliant and comprehensive selection, try *Red Hot Ice Breakers* by Michael Puffett and Sheldon W. Rottler.[8]

Worship time: This can take various forms, depending on your group members and the resources available to you. It may involve some guitar-led singing (so make sure words are visible somehow), or a more creative approach (Try Jenny Baker's *Heart, Soul, Mind, Strength: 50 Creative Worship Ideas for Youth Groups*).[9]

Game: A longer (but not too long) fun activity that links with your session theme. Example: for a session on "putting on the full armour of God" (Ephesians 6), you might give groups a roll of black sacks/bin bags, sticky tape, and a heap of cardboard and invite them to clad one of their number in junk-model armour, with a prize for the best effort.

---

8   Published by Monarch, 1999.
9   Published by Monarch, 2009.

Teaching: You will have a preferred way of doing this, but having a central block of teaching, or at least a time where you raise and open up a theme, is an important central pillar. Don't confuse this with a pulpit, though; ten to fifteen minutes of from-the-front time is plenty.

Small-group Bible study: You may want to look directly at a passage of Scripture (I would advocate doing this regularly), and while you might choose to lead some of this from the front, splitting into smaller groups or even pairs can enable young people to get far more hands-on with the text.

Small-group discussion: Young people are far more likely to open up and share their opinions and ideas in a small group than in a big one. This may link directly to some Bible teaching or exploration, or be more generally focused on the theme. For more discussion starters and group questions than you could ever possibly need, you might want to check out my books *The Ideas Factory* and *The Think Tank*.

Prayer/reflective activity: Don't just teach about a relationship with God – create opportunities for young people to invest in one during the sessions themselves. Get creative; there are 1,001 ways to pray, so work hard not to repeat a familiar style or method week after week.

Recap/conclusion: Like a good sermon or school lesson, a memorable youth session ends with a recap, where you allow members of the group to reflect back what they've learned or explored today. Make sure you plan every session to end a few minutes early to allow for this; it's easy to run out of time (especially when parents are waiting outside), so make sure you prioritize finishing well.

Joining up youth and children's work
Sam Donoghue

Too often, youth work and children's work are seen as utterly separate, with their own unique challenges and opportunities. But this misses something, as a child never crosses a line past which they suddenly become "youth" just as they begin secondary school; we need to join the top end of our children's groups to our youth groups. I hope to explore a little of how these changes look, how we should work in the light of them, and how children's groups should be preparing the way for youth work.

It's easy to think that now the once beautifully mannered children from the Sunday school are forming into a youth group they have become a different species. This is not true; much of what was important then is still important now. A sense of being loved and of belonging is crucial now just as it was in the children's group, and deep inside their experiences of church will still be informing their faith in a foundational way, just as they have been since they were in the crèche. However, there can be no doubt that they are changing, and both children's and youth workers will need to work together to prepare the children for this change and to allow it to deepen their faith, not damage it.

The biggest difference you will see is that they are now able to reflect critically; therefore they will question everything! It is around this time that the stories they accepted when they were younger are being divided into fact and fiction, and God is at risk of joining Santa and the Easter Bunny on the fiction pile. As a youth worker you need to be ready to have these conversations: leading them through the questions and helping them to think about what the answers might be and to develop their own beliefs through them. They are beginning a process that Westerhoff calls "searching faith", and it's very important, as it enables the child to develop their own faith.

However, if we are to try to join our youth work to our children's work we should be helping to initiate this searching in the safety of the church by actively helping children to ask questions early rather than just expecting them to accept everything we say; this means that when they grow into this more questioning phase they are used to church being a place where it's OK to ask a question and that as questions of life develop, the church will be an obvious place to ask them. Too often children are part of Sunday schools where they are spoon-fed and never taught to think for themselves, so they go outside the church with their questions.

I am of the conviction that if we want to have churches filled with teenagers who have their own faith and are able to think for themselves, making good choices, then we need to be teaching them to think for themselves in our children's groups before they join the youth group.

Sam Donoghue is Children's Adviser for the Diocese of London, and one of the founding editors of Childrenswork *magazine. Follow him on Twitter @ SamRDonoghue*

Social programme ideas

As part of your youth work, you may want to run a regular social night which aims both to build community among your existing young people and to create a "safe", non-threatening space for them to bring their mates along to for the first time.

My own experience of youth group as a teenager started in this way – after I had started to explore the Christian faith with a schools worker, he suggested a local church youth group that my friend and I might enjoy. Had this immediately consisted of heavy-duty Bible studies, I probably wouldn't have stayed around for very long. Because the church delivered two related sessions of youth work every weekend (social on Friday, Bible-based programme on Sunday), I was able to make friendships, relax, and "belong" through the Friday group, until after five weeks I decided I would like to spend time with these people on a Sunday night too.

Looking back at it now, I see that the Friday night programme that I grew up with must have required a huge investment of time, planning, and resources from the church's youth ministry team – who at least for the first few years, were all volunteers. Because the work was time consuming, some of the volunteers helped at either one session or the other (although not a huge church, this was one with a particularly large number of people envisioned about youth ministry), and it may be that you simply don't have the resources to run two major meetings per week.

I've also known various youth groups which have run a café-style weekly social night for their faith-focused group. These are effectively the same every week – perhaps given a clubhouse feel, where the young people can drink hot chocolate, buy tuck, play video games, pool, and table football, or some combination thereof. This is a great way of creating a safe space for young people to belong, but I'd suggest that to keep it fresh, you incorporate some changeable element in that – so that there is always an opportunity for members to participate in a different activity each week.

Here are just a few ideas to kick start your planning, if you decide to run a regular social evening:

- **Singing competition** – Perhaps using a games console with a karaoke game.

- **Table-tennis/pool/table football competition** – preferably in teams of two.

- **Regression evening** – Get out paints, modelling dough, potatoes for printing, crayons, and other art materials, and give the group permission to be kids for a night, creating artwork like they used to when they were young.

- **Wide game** – Properly risk-assessed, a game of Capture the Flag or similar played over a large outdoor area, can create fantastic memories.

- **Cooking, baking or cake decoration**.

- **Open mic night** – Where those in the group with a talent for music, stand-up, or something else can perform in front of their friends.

Preparing young people for university
Pippa Elmes

In 2011, stastics showed that 73 per cent of Christian university students don't engage with church[10] – after years of hard graft and faith we lose them as we let them go. So it is vital to lay foundations for longevity and prepare them practically for university.

Being part of a church while at university is essential if Christian young people are to survive this transition and thrive. Unfortunately, finding a church often isn't a priority. While they may identify with a youth group, for many, "church" can still feel alien. We need to raise up students who understand the purpose and call of the church and feel a part of it. From a young age, teach them about "the church" – the body, the bride, the mission plan. Model enthusiasm for our family (however broken) and create opportunities for them to get stuck in. This generation wants to participate, imitate, and innovate. Make serving the body, leading with God-given gifts, and being a valued individual within the family cornerstones of your youth work. Let's celebrate and talk about our church as well as our youth group. If they love, serve, and lead the church at home they will know how to function in and commit to one at uni. Their participation and leadership will also be a real blessing to your church.

Prepare them for life at university. Preparation evenings/days/coffee chats are great. Ask "What are you looking forward to?/What are you nervous about?/Who do you want to be in four years' time?/How might you share your faith with your friends?/What do Christians believe about sex, drunkenness, other religions, and church, and why?" Discuss university culture, giving space for honest reflection. You may be surprised how unaware, or overly aware, your young people are. Encourage them to identify their stumbling blocks, decide on boundaries, and commit to accountability. It's great to have current university students share their experiences too if you can get hold of some! With Student Linkup they can connect to churches and other Christian freshers before leaving home. This time is important for them to take responsibility and think through what lies ahead.

---

10   Christianity and University Experience, 2011.

Going to university is a step into new things, and this should be celebrated. Help them dream big dreams! If they'll let you, commission them in church before they go, sending them off with great hope and encouragement. Pray for God to do greater things than you could ask or imagine and check out Romans 15:13.

Keeping up with students need not be draining. Linking them up with mentors can take the pressure off you. An email in December saying you're looking forward to having them home is a good move, irrespective of what you've seen on Facebook! Allowing them to share their experiences can be done up front, in a newsletter, in a cell group or at dinner with you. Fusion's Studentscape is a cell-group resource you can use if you want to gather them in the holidays.

In all things, let's foster, from the start, a belief that there is always more to discover in God.

Pippa Elmes is Fusion's Student Linkup Developer. Student Linkup connects school leavers to churches and other Christian freshers in their uni towns (www.studentlinkup.org). Email Pippa: pippa@fusion.uk.com or follow her on Twitter @this_is_pip

Further reading

The Ideas Factory – Martin Saunders, Monarch, 2006
The Think Tank – Martin Saunders, Monarch, 2009

6

Nuts and Bolts

So you've planned your first term (right?) – but we're not quite ready to open the shutters just yet. There are still a number of things to think through. This chapter will look at four important areas of youth ministry that you should have addressed and feel confident about before you launch or relaunch your own project. First, we'll look at some of the <u>policies</u> that you should have in place as part of good practice, and in case problems arise. Second, we'll think about how you'll relate to and work in <u>partnership</u> with other youth-service providers in your area. Third, we'll look at the area of <u>supervision</u> – how your work is overseen, and where you can go for support; finally we'll think about <u>boundaries</u>, and how to ensure you maintain a healthy personal life and avoid the classic youth-ministry career-ender, burnout.

Policies and forms

Safeguarding

This is the most important area of youth work to get right, because the safety of the young people in your care must be your first concern. "Safeguarding" is an umbrella term used to describe the processes and procedures that help protect children and others (such as young adults) who might be vulnerable. It might not be particularly glamorous or interesting but it's crucial that you have a safeguarding policy that is fit for purpose and understood by your entire team.

In the UK, the experts in this area are the Churches' Child Protection Advisory Service (CCPAS), which offers a membership package that includes access to an online – and fully searchable – safeguarding manual; model policies and forms; access to training seminars; support from a dedicated team to process disclosure checks, including advising on blemished disclosures; regular email updates, and more.

Its comprehensive advice on safeguarding is summarized in a free booklet, *Safe and Secure: Key Facts*, which can be ordered or downloaded from CCPAS's website, www.ccpas.co.uk. It lists CCPAS's Ten Safeguarding Standards, and acts as a helpful charter document for any church working with children or young people. What follows is a summary of that booklet. But in the long term you should devote serious time to ensuring that everyone in your team has a clear understanding of both your legal responsibilities and best practice in this area. (CCPAS words are in italic, mine in standard type.)

Standard 1: *Organizations should adopt a formal, working safeguarding policy*
This is a government expectation, and means appointing a safeguarding co-ordinator within or relating to your team.

Standard 2: *Organizations must develop safeguarding awareness and provide training*
It's not sufficient for the safeguarding co-ordinator to have all the answers – all youth-work team members should have a working knowledge of safeguarding, and where to go if a concern arises.

Standard 3: *Organizations should adopt a formal recruitment policy for both paid and voluntary workers*

Safer recruitment, including those all-important checks, minimizes the risk of exposing young people to an inappropriate adult.

Standard 4: *Workers, paid and voluntary, should be appropriately managed, supervised, and supported*

We will talk about line management later in the chapter, but good support and teamwork are all part of creating a healthy working atmosphere in which the risk of abuse is minimized. This standard also requires churches to have a proper disciplinary procedure in place for both paid and voluntary staff.

Standard 5: *Organizations must ensure they adopt safe working practice*

Organizations must think about the safety aspect of every organized activity (see section on Risk Assessment below). First Aid provision should also be made, through the training and/or recruitment of First Aiders for the youth-work team.

Standard 6: *Organizations should ensure that workers know how to talk with, listen to, and relate to children with whom they come in contact*

Workers need to be trained to respond appropriately if a young person makes – or appears to make – a disclosure of sensitive information, or simply wants to share something that is troubling them. If your volunteer team know how to relate properly to young people, you immediately have a much better chance of positive, healthy relationships developing between the young people and the team.

Standard 7: *Workers must develop awareness of the issues surrounding abuse, be able to recognize possible signs and symptoms, and respond appropriately*

You must have a safeguarding co-ordinator within your team – even if this person is not regularly involved in your face-to-face youth work – and your whole team should be clear about who this is and how to contact them. This person should then also offer access to (or delivery of) training for the whole team. If there is a disclosure of abuse, or reasonable suspicion that it may be taking place, the safeguarding co-ordinator should be contacted; he or she will then take the matter forward with the relevant external bodies.

Standard 8: *Organizations should ensure pastoral care and support is available to all those affected by abuse*

Abuse is devastating and will have long-term consequences, both for the victim and for those around them. These will include family, friends, and church members. You should seek to be available to listen and offer sensitive support where relevant, recognizing that some people will need professional help in the aftermath of abuse, and helping to implement this where relevant and possible.

Standard 9: *Organizations must supervise and manage those who pose a risk to children*

Your church should have a strong policy in place to ensure that anyone who has previously committed sexual or violent crimes against children is properly supervised and managed. You must check that this is in place, and understand any role that you may have to play within it.

Standard 10: *Organizations working in specialized areas, culturally diverse settings or through partner organizations or agencies must ensure appropriate safeguarding policies and procedures are in place*

Specifically, while we should be sensitive to cultural or religious traditions, these should never be allowed to "condone practices which are harmful, abusive or neglectful".

If you find yourself in a difficult or potentially dangerous safeguarding situation, call CCPAS's twenty-four-hour helpline on 0845 120 45 50.

E-safety policy

It is vitally important that your church/organization has an e-safety policy, especially with regard to your interaction with children. Advances in technology have brought with them a whole new wave of risks for children and young people, and you have a responsibility to ensure that your work does not expose them to any of those risks. A working e-safety policy should contain detailed and carefully thought-out references to the following areas:

Social media

Had this book been written just ten years ago, this section would make no sense. Yet the advent of social media has brought one of the biggest shifts in the nature of youth culture(s) in history. Many young people do the majority of their socializing from the comfort and supposed safety of their own bedroom. Yet the reality is that this can often be far from the safe place that it seems to be. Adults with an inappropriate interest in children and young people will use social networking and online discussion tools such as Facebook, Twitter, Chat Roulette, chat rooms, and webcam sites to attempt to make contact and form connections with under-sixteens.

Not only that – many adults working with children and young people in an appropriate context such as education or youth work have made serious errors of judgment when connecting with them in a digital space. The consequences of such a mistake could range from a slap across the wrist for a breach of good practice, to a prison sentence for starting a sexual affair with a minor which began with an online conversation. This is serious stuff.

Because these phenomena are still relatively new, and because the social media platforms themselves continue to evolve rapidly, hard-and-fast rules are sketchy. Sites such as Facebook have a minimum user age (currently thirteen), and the serious offline consequences of online connection – such as under-age sexual activity – of course remain illegal. Yet there are huge grey areas within the online space, and with most young people now able to access the internet through several devices at home and on the move, it's vital not only that you help young people to understand the risks they face in the digital world, but that you also have a policy in place for the way that your youth-ministry team relates to young people online.

Use of images (photographic and video)

You may want to use images of young people in your publicity, or on a website; you may even want to have some video content on the latter. In principle this isn't a bad idea – after all, people will feel much more relaxed about attending (or allowing their children to attend) a new activity if they can see what it looks like. However, if you do publish photographs of children or young people under sixteen, you must have obtained written parental permission beforehand. A simple uniform typed statement, signed and dated by a parent/guardian of each child involved, will suffice. Failure to do this could leave you extremely vulnerable to legal action from an unhappy parent, if they did not consent in writing to your use of their child's image.

Email

As you consider your e-safety policy, you should also consider how to make any email communication between yourself and the young people clear, appropriate, and unambiguous. You might also think about obtaining some form of parental consent for you to email young people, or to make it your practice always to copy in their parents to any email dialogue. I would suggest that you use email only as a mechanism for getting news out, rather than using it to get involved in lengthy conversations with individuals. To this end, you may want to set up a generic account for the youth-work team, for which several DBS-checked team members have access and shared responsibility. You should also make it a matter of policy not to delete any emails sent or received (this is no problem for a high-capacity provider like www.gmail.com), just in case the worst happens.

Mobile phones

You should also have a policy for your interaction with young people via mobile phone. Remember that nowadays many mobiles are as powerful and functional as fully-equipped computers; they're also wirelessly connected to the internet and, of course, they work as phones. What an incredible communications package! Mobile devices are the chief way that many people access the internet, especially when the content they are looking for is of a "sensitive" nature.

Because mobile phones allow 24/7 access to a young person, they are unfortunately open to abuse from adults (and other young people) acting with inappropriate intent. For this reason above all others, you should ensure that you have parental consent before you contact an under-sixteen (best practice: under-eighteen) via SMS or phone call. It may be that you are able to obtain consent to communicate with your young people via a range of media, through a single signed form.

Risk assessments

A risk assessment is exactly what it sounds like. Before undertaking any new activity or taking the group on a trip, you should complete a risk assessment form. It may be that you will submit this to your line manager in advance of some activity taking place; it is more likely you will simply use it to influence your approach to an activity, and keep it to refer to later if necessary. Again, this isn't the most exciting or inspiring element of working with young people, but safety is paramount. When minors are left in your care, you are responsible and liable for returning them to their parents in one piece.

Here is an example of a risk assessment form. You can develop your own form based on this template, or obtain templates from a variety of sources such as the Health and Safety Executive (www.hse.gov.uk) and CCPAS. I have filled in an example to illustrate what is expected.

Hazard	Who might be harmed and how?	What can you do in advance to manage this risk?	What can you do to minimize risks during activity?	Who is responsible for taking action?	Action by when?	Done
Travelling by minibus	Young people and leaders could be injured by unsafe driving or poor onboard safety	Ensure minibus driver has experience and appropriate licence	Young people briefed to wear seatbelts; this will be reinforced on board	MS	1/10/12	1/10/12

Although you will need to complete a risk assessment for new activities and trips, don't forget that you should complete one for your regular work and venue(s) too. In this case, you might like to replace the third column heading with "What are you already doing?", and the fourth with "Do you need to do anything else to manage this risk?" since this activity will be ongoing.

Partnership

Youth work doesn't take place in a vacuum.

Your ministry is likely to operate within (or at least under the oversight of) a church; which in turn is situated in a local community. That community will, in the vast majority of cases, also contain other groups and individuals seeking to engage, provide for or protect young people.

So you have a decision to make (and forgive me for lodging my tongue in my cheek): do you think that your brand of youth ministry is so unique, so holistic, and so much better than that of all those other people who are getting it subtly wrong, that you should operate as an island, never seeking to connect with – for want of a better word – your rival youth providers? Or, instead, do you believe that there could be merit in building partnerships with those who share your concern and care for young people?

Local churches have not always been brilliant at working with each other. Yet in recent years (thanks in part to the rise of city-wide and even nationwide cross-denominational mission initiatives) this picture has improved, particularly among youth workers. I regularly hear of gatherings taking place in local communities, usually over food and around a commitment to pray, where youth leaders from across the denominational divides get together every so often to share stories and dream together. Out of meetings like that, initiatives and events grow, as those youth workers realize that their peers have the same dreams for the young people of that community that they do.

And perhaps they've realized something else: in any local community, the members of any one church, heading off to attend their service on a given Sunday, look like a strange and disparate group of perhaps a hundred people. Yet if on the same Sunday all the members of all the churches in that community were to simultaneously leave their homes and congregate in its centre, this would suddenly constitute a small army of local believers.

The same is true for young people – so I want to encourage you not only to build relationships with other local youth workers and churches, but to look for every opportunity to work in partnership with them. When you do this, you pool – and therefore increase – your resources, and you create experiences for young people that teach them about a united body and enable them to see that they are not alone.

Unity... from scratch
Ali Campbell

All around you there just might be some allies who will enable you to do more than you have yet imagined is possible – and they are the other churches in your area. There is the church we see (ours, the local Catholic, Anglican, Methodist, Baptist, or whatever) and then there is the church Jesus sees – the whole church, all of us: every follower of Jesus.

Ephesians 4 lays it out for us: one faith, one Lord, one hope. A quite famous Christian has said that "the hope for the world is the local church". While our church might be our spiritual home, the hope is to be found in Jesus himself; our activity with young people needs to point to Him, be about Him, and be for Him. If our focus is on growing our church, we can miss some essential aspects of what we need to share and demonstrate to the next generation.

Here, then, are my reasons why, if it is possible where you are, you should work with across the churches to engage with young people, introduce them to Jesus and nurture faith:

Where there is unity, God commands a blessing. It is not about huge amazing numbers of young people. Blessing comes through shared endeavour, relationships being built, and our understanding of the breadth of worship and practice across the church.

Others are more likely to know we are followers of Jesus. In John 17, Jesus prays that we might be one – that the world might know that we are His disciples. Jesus knew how much we would need each other; working with others from different churches makes it more likely that we seek to grow the kingdom rather than an empire, and makes it less likely that one ego or charismatic person takes the focus away from Jesus.

The young people you work with are unlikely to be in your church as adults. We live in a global village; connections are made, by many young people, all over the world, every day. Their world is huge; they are exposed to all kinds of things (for good or ill). When they grow up and move away, the chances of their finding a church just like yours are tiny. However, if through working with others you have exposed them to different kinds of church, different forms of worship, etc., they are more likely to find a spiritual home with some of the things they recognize.

They don't care about growing up "Baptist"... or whatever happens to be your church denomination. Think about that for a minute. Do the young people you know who are Christians talk about being Anglican or Baptist – or evangelical or liberal or catholic? Probably not – they're just Christians!

Young people are already doing stuff together. A lot of the young people who live in a community with a few churches in it might well be in one school. They know each other, work together, and see each other every day; this is unlike the experience of adults in our local churches, who probably don't all work at the same office! We need to start where young people are, rather than from our default "church" place.

How, then, do you start? The following six things are all possible for any church. Give these a go, and begin to see a difference in your approach and engagement with young people.

1. Resources. You, as a youth worker, volunteer, or other leader are an amazing resource – your stories, your life, your faith. Each church in your community has a great resource in its people. Begin there. Then start to look together at what resources you might be able to pool for the common good.

2. Relationships. When wanting to "do" something together we can often overlook the importance of investing in relationships for their own sake. Getting to know others is vital if those things we want to "do" are going to be done with less misunderstanding and mistrust. The better we know the people in another church, the better we will be able to work together.

3. Pray. Nothing brings closer unity than prayer. Jesus is not talking about prayer in John 17, He is praying about and for unity. Pray for the church up the road; pray for what they are doing; pray that God will bless their leaders and grow their church. Mean it, too.

4. Communicate. This sounds obvious, but do you know what they "do" up the road? Communication makes a big difference to whether you duplicate effort, or complement each other and recognize each church's unique contribution.

5. Co-ordinate. Get the other things going nicely and you can think about what you might do together and then co-ordinate that work. School assemblies might work best if there is co-ordinated effort; in a school an after-school club might work better, and be more sustainable, if you did it together. Holiday Clubs, Social Action Projects, Acts of Witness – all of which can involve young people – are so much better done together!

6. Shared youth work. What would it look like if, across your area, youth provision came from a shared youth-work project? What if the young people from your church went to a discipleship group that was near where they lived, rather than across town, because the churches were running them together? What if you organized a weekend away together (the more people you take, the cheaper these can be for everyone)? What if there were a termly celebration of all the youth work in the town where stories were shared, young people and their leaders were prayed for, and where the churches the young people were in acted as the one church that Jesus sees?

Ali Campbell is the Youth and Children's Adviser for the Diocese of Chichester. Follow him on twitter: @alicampbellyes

Other churches and Christian organizations are a great place to start when you're thinking about partnership, but they're by no means the only place. If you really want to have an impact on your local community, you may want to think about discovering, meeting, and even working with other local people and groups who are offering provision for, or take a particular interest in, young people. These might include:

- **Local, statutory-run youth work:** including drop-in clubs, mentoring schemes, and detached workers. These local youth workers – in the UK greatly reduced in number after waves of government cuts – share a great deal of your heart for young people. They may not be particularly interested in leading teenagers to Jesus, but like you they are concerned for their holistic welfare. If you are able to find a way of working together – for instance on a shared initiative such as an open youth club – then you may begin to see each other as allies, rather than rivals.

- **The police:** Just as with every generation, there will be some young people locally who choose to engage in risky or even illegal behaviour. Building good relationships with the local police creates a two-way street, through which you can seek one another's help, and even have the opportunity to mediate in difficult situations involving young people. In most cases, local police forces are extremely positive about any project that occupies young people in positive activities, so this may be more of an open door than you imagine, and may even lead to partnership on informal education or other initiatives.

- **Local charities and sports clubs:** These are not rivals for young people's attention – although inevitably some young people will choose to play football or get involved in an awards scheme that will clash with church – but rather should be seen as potential partners. Could you develop an initiative which complements their activities? The first step is always to meet the people involved.

Partnership working... from scratch

Andy Burns

I must confess to being a born-again "partnerist". My journey in partnering with statutory bodies such as borough councils, schools, police, and youth development services has enabled my youth-ministry dreams to be realized. As you start out on your journey, I want to encourage you to see youth work not purely as a church community activity, but rather as an activity in the community where God is already active. So here are a few thoughts that I want to pass on:

1. Own your mission. This is essential, as it frames what you can and should partner in. This is a vital point to grasp, as partnership stands a chance of working only when we know what we are offering, what our focus is, and where our boundaries lie. For example, the charity that I work for is, at its missional core, a pastoral and compassionate response to young people. This means that we can work collaboratively with a wide variety of partners in the area of youth well-being: pastoral care, counselling, housing, advice, and guidance. Where we struggle to deliver is when we venture off-piste into areas that are outside our focus and skill sets.

2. Remember the drivers. Always be mindful that what drives you in youth work maybe different from what motivates your statutory partners. A few years ago we had a contract with our local authority to address teenage unemployment (a big driver for them), and we were commissioned to meet the need by addressing the well-being of those who were unemployed (a big driver for us); partnership was therefore possible. However, in time the drive simply to address unemployment rather than their pastoral needs became so great that we had to cancel the contract. Protect what brings you to the table of partnership: your missional focus and your driver is what makes you prophetically distinctive.

3. Focus on what unites. The key to partnership working is the need to embrace what unites us in youth work and not to focus on what divides. A good biblical framework for partnership working can be found in Jeremiah 29:7: "Seek the peace of the city", and in Luke 10:6, where Jesus instructs his disciples to "find the person of peace". In seeking the peace and finding the person of peace, we are partnering on what matter to us all, on what we all long to see. Both church and society want to see happy, whole, healthy, achieving, loved, and thriving young people. We may use different language: "Let Your kingdom come" to you translates as "Add value" to a head teacher; "Community cohesion" to a Chief Inspector; and, "Community transformation" to a councillor. More often than not it's the language that divides us, not the dreams we corporately have for young people.

So, practically, how do you start?

Ask to meet a local councillor and explore how you can work together; don't see them simply as a meal ticket. Book an appointment with your local head teacher; bring an attitude of service and see where that leads. Is the local youth centre struggling? Then see if you can volunteer. Start listening to what the need is; watch your language, speak English not Christianese, and allow yourself time to understand Statutory-speak. Be normal; overly bouncy Christians are not always trusted; passion for young people and eccentricity are two very different things.

The most important thing I've learned, however, is that people partner with people; relationships built on trust last and prosper longer than contracts. Be committed to seeking the peace and finding the person of peace, and enjoy the kingdom coming.

Andy Burns runs the charity East2West. Follow him on twitter @andyburns1974, and visit his blog: http://love-is-youthwork.posterous.com

Supervision

Youth work is never a lone-wolf endeavour – or, at least, it shouldn't be. Horror stories abound of well-intentioned people who, freed from spiritual or practical accountability, have fallen into disastrous (or at least wayward) practice because they didn't have someone looking out for them. Of course, that's not really freedom at all – operating without supervision is, for anyone with a conscience, the route to extreme pressure and stress.

I would like to suggest that anyone planning to run a youth-ministry initiative should be able to look up to two independent sources of supervision (the temptation will be to tie these together in a single person – resist it). The first is a professional supervisor – a line manager, if you like; the second is a mentor or spiritual director whose interest is solely in how you, as the leader, are managing to live out your own faith while you seek to disciple others in it.

I know of a church where an unsupervised, unmanaged youth worker ended up going to prison because of a sexual relationship with a fifteen-year-old in his care. While that behaviour is entirely indefensible, it is worth noting that the support structure around this young man was virtually non-existent. The church – a large and flourishing one – brought him in effectively to "solve" their youth-work "problem" (it was non-existent). He was young, trendy, charismatic, and dynamic – and so the church leadership perceived that he already possessed the entire arsenal required for a successful youth-ministry initiative. They could "set him loose to pioneer". He built a group quickly because he was great at cultivating relationships, and then he got one of those badly wrong. Had he reported to a line manager, his work patterns would probably have been questioned; had he been spiritually mentored, he might well have confessed to inappropriate feelings before things got out of hand. We don't know for sure. What we do know is that – saddled with the false liberation of lone-wolf youth work – he made a devastating mistake.

Not every story of poor or non-existent supervision ends like this – of course it's the extreme and, thankfully, exceptional case. Yet there are many other pitfalls in working unaccountably, and avoiding them is worth what might sometimes feel like the downside. When you're supervised properly, you will inevitably be told (or at least strongly advised) not to do some things. Since none of us possesses the wisdom of Solomon, this is a better thing than we give it credit for. When you're meeting regularly with an involved line manager, you will be asked to consider doing things you might not have chosen to do, or to explore different ways of working that might not come naturally. Assuming that your line manager is acting with integrity, embrace this.

So what do these two strands of supervision look like in practice?

"Line-manager" supervision

There seem to be a lot of unattributed statistics in the church about the length of time that professional youth workers stay in an average post, and in youth ministry per se. As the worst of sinners – as someone who has quoted numbers like "eighteen months and out" from conference stages – can I confess: I'm not sure any of us actually knows the reality. Any research that has been done in this area has involved small, biased samples. All we can do is take an educated, anecdotal guess – and it goes something like this:

Churches that employ youth workers (you may not be employed, but bear with me) generally fall into two camps. First, there are those who claim not to understand young people, or youth ministry, and who bring in youth workers as "fixers" to rescue their ageing congregational demographic. They believe that these youth workers – complete with cape and underpants outside trousers – know what they're doing, have the answers, and – since they speak a different language anyway – are best left to their own devices. In my fairly extensive experience, these youth workers don't last very long. Burdened with expectation and without a safe outlet for concerns and frustrations, they feel unsupported and misunderstood. Before long, the jobs pages at the back of *Youthwork* magazine become more and more enticing.

The second camp in this wonderfully generalized diagram is made up of churches that "get it". They understand that a youth worker, just like an assistant minister or worship pastor, is a part of the team and, even more fundamentally than that, a human being. The leaders of such churches invest time in meeting, talking with, showing interest in, and even helping the youth worker. They understand that they – or someone else in the team – have "line-management" responsibility for that person. That's not "line oversight"; it's not some detached idea that sounds good in the church AGM. Rather, it's an involved, two-way relationship which gives both parties space to express concerns, praise, and frustrations, and to share both good and bad news. It's a mechanism through which concerns can be identified and resolved early, rather than being left to fester into a problem which ends in the youth worker leaving. Again, I have no statistics, but *all* the youth workers I know who have stayed in a post for a considerable time have enjoyed this kind of relationship.

So (volunteers, I hope you're still with me), what does this look like in practice? I'd like to suggest that, whether you're a full-timer or a lead volunteer, it is vital that you report to some sort of line manager who has an interest both in you and in the direction and health of the youth work. A semi-formal meeting (by which I mean you're relaxed, but taking it seriously) on a regular basis will enable you to go helpfully through the process of reporting back on the state of the youth work. As a full-timer this might be for an hour every other week – as a lead volunteer perhaps this would happen two or three times a term. As you establish your relationship you may want to devise your own content and pattern for these meetings, but, as a starting point, the worksheet below will give you some helpful conversation triggers (you may find it helpful either to fill the sheet in at the meeting or to make some notes on the relevant points beforehand).

You may want to adapt this, but I hope it gives an idea of what a balanced conversation might look like. You'll notice that the meeting is in two parts – I would expect neither of these to be a monologue, but certainly they will be driven by the relevant person – avoiding a dysfunctional meeting where one person is driving and dominating. This way, both get space to speak. The point labelled "Upward review" is simply an opportunity for the youth minister to raise any concerns (or express thanks) about the way they are being managed.

Agenda for lead youth minister/line manager meeting

Date: _____   Date of last meeting: _____

- Opening prayer

A) The youth minister

- Report back on news/progress in the youth-ministry area since last meeting

- Issues/concerns raised previously – update

- New issues/concerns to raise

- Upward review

B) The line manager

- Issues/concerns raised previously – update

- New issues/concerns to raise

- Report on relevant news affecting wider church (or organization)

- Set date of next meeting

- Closing prayer

A good line-management relationship not only makes for better youth work – it also empowers the youth minister and gives them prominence as a vital part of the operation. In a church, a positive line manager can be your advocate to the rest of the leadership and congregation, and will join with you in fighting to ensure that youth ministry is properly understood, prayed for, and funded by the church as a whole.

Spiritual supervision

This is a very different relationship, and one which I would suggest exists outside the boundaries of the church you serve. Many terms exist for this form of supervision (and all mean slightly different things): mentor, spiritual director, accountability partner, and more. What all of them have in common, however, is that the focus is on you, not the youth work.

Do not be so proud (it's a misplaced humility) as to assume that you don't need someone to look out for you. Someone who doesn't have a vested interest in your "output" (not a parent – NEVER a parent); someone who is "for" you, and who wants to see you both succeed and grow in your relationship with God. This is the youth-work equivalent of the trainer in a boxer's corner who puts his fighter's health first and is prepared to throw in the towel to protect him – everyone needs a person whose first concern is not what they do, but who they are. The trainer knows that one more punch will do his friend serious damage – even if he can't see it for himself. In the same way, a spiritual supervisor is able to look at the honest big picture of our lives (which includes, but isn't only about, our work) and help us to see what we're sometimes unable to see for ourselves.

I would strongly suggest that you build personal retreat time into the rhythm of your year (more on your own spiritual disciplines in the "Boundaries" section), but, alongside that, meeting regularly with a spiritual supervisor could be a vital key to your long-term ministry and well-being. Find someone who is older than you (as regards spiritual maturity at least), whom you trust, respect, and know to be "for" you. This can't – I should stress this is only a strong opinion – be a peer who is going for the same life goals as you. It needs to be someone whom you feel you can learn from, and from whom you would be prepared to take even severe constructive criticism. Ask this person if they are prepared to meet with you for at least a year (which gives enough time for the relationship to deepen), ideally every month, otherwise at least once every two months. If you are meeting less frequently, try to make the sessions longer – a whole evening instead of a coffee and catch-up.

When you meet, use the first few sessions to get to know each other and to ensure that it is possible to build a deep, high-trust relationship with this person. After that, if the relationship functions well, I would suggest you devote some of your time together to praying and listening to God, some to talking through concerns and situations that have arisen in your youth work, and then some time looking at a Bible passage. This might see you working through a Gospel or one of Paul's letters together, or it might be that you deliberately focus on different passages that talk about Christlike leadership characteristics – perseverance, integrity, joy, service, and so on. Doing this will ensure not only that you spend some time immersed in Scripture for yourself (rather than in the process of planning a youth talk!), but also that your relationship with your spiritual supervisor will naturally deepen through the discipline of studying God's living word together.

When it comes to establishing your youth ministry (or rebooting something), don't make this the final thing on your to-do list, which never gets done. I've moved house twice, and each time I left behind unfinished DIY jobs that were really quite important, and which I never got round to. In both cases, the value of what I had to sell was affected. In the same way, making sure you have a person looking out for your spiritual health is the sort of job that is easy to excuse away, but which will create problems if left undone. If possible, recruit this "spiritual supervisor" before you ever put out the beanbags for your first youth drop-in.

Accountability

Matt Summerfield

It was G.K. Chesterton who once said, *"Christianity has not been tried and found wanting; it's been found difficult and not tried."* Even for those of us who embrace the faith, we're all very much aware of our continuing struggles. Wrong thoughts, words, and actions desperately try to drag us back to an old life and it's so tempting to keep that stuff hidden – just between us and God. Stupid! I've seen too many people crash in their lives because they were struggling with some secret sin that they never had the courage to speak about.

The Scriptures make it very clear that we need God's continuing power in our lives, and yet God is not enough. Yes, you did hear that right! After all, it was God who said that in Genesis 2:18. He says, *"It is not good for the man to be alone. I will make a helper suitable for him."* God knows we need Him, but we also need others.

So, if we are serious about becoming fully devoted followers of Jesus Christ, then we all need honest, authentic, vulnerable, accountable relationships where we help each other live out God's best way. In fact, I would go as far as to say that you will **never** fully realize your full potential in Jesus Christ without a handful of Christians around you who love you enough to speak words of challenge and discipline into your life – while you do the same for them.

So where do you start? Perhaps the answer is as simple as 1–2–3.

Why not invite ONE person to be your "guide"? Someone you're learning from. Someone who can help and challenge you to become everything that God created you to be. What matters is that you give them permission to listen and speak into your life.

Then why not ask at least TWO people to be your "running mates"? People whom you share your life with, being open about your real struggles, your secret life – people who will help you put into practice the challenges from your "guide".

Finally, what if you were willing to pass on the baton of faith to THREE other people? Equipping them to become all that God created them to be, inspiring each of them to share their faith with others. Disciples making disciples.

The apostle Paul understood the importance of these kinds of relationships. In 2 Timothy 2:2, he writes, "You have heard me teach things that have been confirmed by many reliable witnesses. Now teach these truths to other trustworthy people who will be able to pass them on to others" (NLT).

So commit yourself to live life 1–2–3. Pray that God will show you who these people could be, set expectations, agree how often you'll meet, how open will you be – and then just do it! You'll be thankful that you did.

Matt Summerfield is the National Director of Urban Saints. Find out more about Live Life 1–2–3 at: www.livelife123.org

Boundaries

Giving yourself to youth ministry shouldn't mean giving up on the life you once lived. When my wife and I had our beautiful, wonderful (they're asleep as I write this) children, we said goodbye to the high life of restaurants, nights out, and lazy Saturday mornings that we'd led when we first got married. We have had to sacrifice the lifestyle we used to enjoy, because of our commitment to looking after our children. The same shouldn't apply to youth ministry. You may want to make yourself available to young people; you may even tell them that in a crisis or emergency, but ultimately your work with teenagers will be much poorer if you never have any space carved out for yourself.

Whether you're a full-time youth minister, or a volunteer able to offer a few hours of your time each week, you can fall victim to youth-ministry burnout. Here's why: youth ministry is rewarding and addictive; as you become more involved in the lives of young people – in making a difference to them or becoming their trusted guide – you will become increasingly committed to them. At the same time, they will increasingly trust and respect you, and – when necessary – seek your time. So as your relationships with young people deepen, so does the potential time commitment and the emotional energy expended in helping, caring for, and praying for them.

I know of a volunteer youth leader whose marriage very nearly broke down over this issue. Dave (let's call him that) worked full-time in a demanding job, but also gave up two nights of every week to run the youth work at his church. He led a team of volunteers like him, organized the programmes – even appointed young people to lead midweek cell groups, and met with those young leaders regularly to check on them. Because he was organized (and because he had access to his office photocopier!), he managed to keep this up for a couple of years, and while his wife wasn't interested in becoming involved in the youth ministry, she was broadly supportive of what he was doing.

When the youth work became more successful, however, Dave got himself into trouble. With evangelistic opportunities springing up, Dave was keen to seize on them; with the group growing, he was eager to invest in more and more young people. As they grew to love him, the teenagers in the group came to him more and more often – sometimes even late at night – for advice or for prayer. Dave's life became more and more frenetic. Something had to give, and since it couldn't be his job, two other areas took the strain – his relationships (principally with his wife, but also with friends), and his own walk with God.

On the outside, it looked as if Dave was thriving, but on the inside he was struggling. He knew that he was barely finding time to pray or read the Bible for himself; his stress levels were rising; he and his wife were seeing less and less of each other, and, when they were together, they fought. He felt hugely conflicted: how could doing something as positive as caring for young people cause so many problems?

Eventually things came to a head, as Dave's wife gave him an ultimatum: it was her or the youth ministry. Dave made the difficult – but correct – decision to step down from his involvement in the church's youth ministry, which had a significant effect on the young people.

What Dave (still married, happily, and a lot wiser) now realizes is that he should have put better boundaries in place, both for himself and with the young people in his care. He says that he should have prioritized better, and not tried to do quite so much before he'd grown a leadership team that could deliver a lot of the ministry without him. He also admits that he had given young people the impression that they could call on him day or night, and that part of this at least was about feeding his own ego and need to feel important.

I don't know what you take out of a story like this, but, as "Dave" suggests, it's very important to continually reassess your priorities. Take out a pen and paper now, and list all the areas of responsibility and activity in your life. This list might include:

• Your relationship or marriage
• Any children
• Your relationship with God
• Your job
• Your involvement in youth ministry
• Key friendships
• Hobbies and interests
• Other church involvement.

Now, as you look at that list, try to order it in importance. The top two in the list above are probably a good place to start – but, after that, be really honest – you may surprise yourself. After you've done this, in a different colour or using a different marking, order these priorities into the amount of time and energy you commit to them. Be really honest! You may find that this exercise is deeply revealing. After completing it, pray – asking God to help you to get your priorities in the right order, and decide on any action you might need to take, such as dropping something, or investing more in an area, in order to become more balanced.

Protecting your relationships

As the previous story proves, youth ministry can have a seriously detrimental effect on relationships if we overcommit ourselves. While there are many stories of husband-and-wife teams finding great joy in each other through serving together in youth work, there are equally situations where one partner invests him- or herself hugely in young people, and the other becomes more and more resentful as that task begins to take up more and more time.

This is doubly true for couples who also have children. A friend of mine grew up as the daughter of a much-loved church youth worker. Her mum's ministry thrived for many years, and during that time hundreds of teenagers were discipled in the Christian faith. Yet one of those young people grew up feeling sad, and eventually bitter, about this – her daughter. Why? Because, while her mum always had time for teenagers, she felt like the lowest and last priority – even when she was a teenager herself. Other people's children got care, attention, and laughter; she got shouted at for bad behaviour and told to do chores. Her mother's own child came last.

So here's the important thing: your own marriage, and your own children – if indeed you have either – are your first concern. A healthy personal life is one of the two key components (I'll come to the second in a moment) that provide a platform for a healthy and successful youth minister. Take care of them; prioritize them; make them understand and feel that they are more important to you than anything.

For that reason, whether you're a full-time youth worker or a gas fitter who helps with your church's youth ministry, it's vital that you build dedicated, special family time into your week, and at least one evening of quality time for your marriage. A lot of people call the latter a "date night" – time when you're intentionally investing in one another, having fun together, talking about things that matter, and, crucially, not watching television.

If you're not married, then you should still carve out this time in your week, to spend either with a boyfriend or girlfriend, if you have one, or else with good friends who understand, love, and re-energize you.

This may all sound patronizing – forgive me if it does – but I have seen too many good youth workers fail to stick to these very simple principles of balance and routine, with results ranging from unhelpful to tragic.

Developing spiritual disciplines
Steve Griffiths

A few years back, my wife and I bought a derelict property to rebuild and do up from scratch. It would become, over a period of two years, our dream house. I'm not going to tell you how much we had planned to spend on it – but, even now, I break out in a sweat just thinking about that! Because we were putting so much money and energy into the project, we wanted to see the results as quickly as we could. But the first eight months were a real disappointment; it seemed as if the builders were just digging holes, knocking walls down, and putting in place things below ground (such as foundations and pipes and electrical cables) that we would never see again. All this work was taking place, but there was nothing tangible to see. However, when the house was finally finished, we realized that the first eight months of "invisible" work were actually the most important of all.

Starting a new youth work, or re-energizing an old one, is a difficult task. There is so much to do, so much to plan, so many demands on your time. But the key lesson I have learned from twenty-five years of

Christian ministry is that it is the "invisible" work of laying strong spiritual foundations that determines how we are able to cope with the physical, emotional, and spiritual demands of ministry.

When it comes to developing spiritual disciplines, many youth workers make the mistake of seeing this as "one more thing to do": the quiet time, prayer, fasting, and tithing are more demands on an already busy schedule. But I want to challenge you, from the Benedictine tradition, to see it a little differently...

Here's the difference between the Benedictine tradition and how most of us operate most of the time.

We tend to see our "work" as all the things we have to do: planning sessions, pastoral care, administration, etc. When we have finished our work, we find time to slot in some prayer and quiet time with God...

In the Benedictine tradition, our "work" is prayer and quiet time with God. When we have finished our work, we then undertake the tasks of the day: planning sessions, pastoral care, administration, etc. The Benedictine tradition turns on its head the outdated, overworked, and unsuccessful notion that our lives are made up of both "work" and "spiritual discipline". Rather, spiritual discipline *is* our work – and everything else is secondary.

It seems to me that spiritual disciplines are the key to staying sane in Christian ministry. But we don't want to see them as an extra "thing" we have to do. What we need is a mind-shift; to recognize that spending time with God is our real work – it is what we were made for, it is our destiny – and everything else comes after that and flows out from that.

It is an enormous challenge to shift our thinking in this way. There is a real temptation to go back to the old way of thinking after a few days, or months, or weeks, when the pressures of ministry begin to build. But I would urge you to persevere and see the difference emerge in your own life. You will understand yourself differently. You will see God differently. You will see your ministry from a new perspective. And, crucially, you will avoid the burnout that so often hits youth workers who still believe that their "work" is "to do" and have missed the point of their very existence: to worship God and spend time in his presence.

Revd Dr Steve Griffiths is a former Director of Cambridge Centre for Youth Ministry, and Rector of Linton Team ministry. Follow him on Twitter @StMarysLinton

Prioritizing your spiritual life

The second element of that "platform" I described in the last section is your own walk with God. Again, forgive me if this comes across as patronizing – my experience tells me that it is worth addressing.

I remember running into a very high-profile Christian leader while we were both in the United States, and having a very unexpected conversation with him on this subject. He was just about to address a huge conference crowd, and so I would have expected him to look energized; nervous, perhaps, but certainly excited. He made a confession: "I've been speaking all around the world for the last few months, and I realized this morning, I haven't sat down and talked with the Father through all that time." It was a moment of searing honesty which any of us in Christian leadership can connect with on some level; sometimes we get so caught up in leading and discipling others that we neglect our own continuing discipleship journey.

I know that there have been times when I've preached the virtues of regular devotional times to young people while my own have either been rushed, sparse, or non-existent. It's not enough to take the "do as I say, don't do as I do" approach – we disciple out of our own discipleship.

It's important, then, that we build investment into our relationship with God, into the regular rhythms of our life. Rather than simply suggesting that you commit to a regular prayer and Bible time, however (as virtuous as those are), I would again encourage you to explore all the ancient spiritual disciplines in order to discover tools that genuinely help you to connect with God.

Read Richard Foster's *Celebration of Discipline*. Or, if you're secretly after the ...*for Dummies* version, then look at the leader's notes which constitute about half of my book *The Beautiful Disciplines*, which look both at how to teach the disciplines to young people and how to explore them in your own life.

We've already talked a little about your own spiritual life in the section on supervision, but I'm repeating myself intentionally. I once asked a very well-known Anglican minister if he would consider being my spiritual director. I must now confess that I made that request with entirely the wrong motive – I was secretly hoping to be able to dazzle people with the revelation that this man was my mentor (yes, I'm an idiot). In that wonderful, gentle-but-firm way that elderly vicars can have, he rejected the request outright, but while he may have perceived my wonky motives, the reason he gave was a brilliant one.

"If I become your spiritual director," he said, "then you'll start to build your spiritual life with me. You'll build a holy relationship with me, not with God. I'll get in the way." He told me he didn't believe in spiritual directors, and, while I still don't agree with him, I took a very clear lesson from that conversation. A spiritual supervisor must never become your high priest. He or she should never replace God as the one you come to with your concerns, thankfulness, and – most fundamentally – prayers.

The point is this: even if you've followed my suggestions about spiritual supervision to the letter, don't allow yourself to believe that the "spiritual health" element of your youth ministry has been covered. As I've said before, your discipleship of young people comes out of your own discipleship – not with a minister or supervisor, but with Jesus himself.

Taking up the call, the challenge, and the privilege of youth ministry means recommitting yourself to your own walk with God. It means taking seriously the responsibility to pray and meet with God regularly (Paul suggests we should "pray continually" in 1 Thessalonians 5:17). It means committing ourselves to reading, studying, and meditating on Scripture so that we might gain enough understanding to teach and explore it with young people.

Why is this little sermon housed in a section headed "Boundaries"? Because, in the pressured, frenetic, multi-priority existence of youth ministry, our spiritual life – just like our personal life – often seems to be the easiest element to compromise and trash-compact. If we don't prioritize our spiritual life, building in disciplines and rhythms that ensure we give it proper attention, it will wither away, and, sadly, so might we.

So, then, just as we carve out a "date night" to spend time with a loved one, or protect time to see important friends, build in some ring-fenced, quality time (so not at 11 p.m.) to spend with the God for whom we do all this, and in whose power we hope to see young lives changed.

Boundaries and burnout
Matt Costley

I had been working full-time in youth ministry for eight years when I hit a wall. It's not like there was a crisis at church; in fact, the youth ministry was growing, thriving even. The teenagers were loving it, other leaders were happy and envisioned, the vicar was happy... yet I was burnt out and was signed off work for several months. I spent a lot of time resting, praying, and reflecting, and realized that my lack of "boundaries" (a word I hated then and still do not love today!) meant that I was finding my identity more in my role as a "youth pastor" than I was as a follower of Jesus. That was bad news for my faith, for my marriage, and for my family. So how can we get it right? How can we stay in youth ministry for the long haul? Is there such a thing as an "on-duty" or "off-duty" youth worker?

Ministry, and youth ministry in particular, is an area where the idea of having boundaries can feel inherently wrong. Hopefully, we believe we are called by God to this ministry and to this role, and because we have given our lives to Christ we want to give our lives to the young people too. It is entirely natural that we should worry about them, about the daily decisions they make, and of course about their eternal destiny. After all, some would say that Jesus didn't seem to have boundaries; He simply gathered a group of young people and spent three years eating, sleeping, travelling, and "doing life" with them – what we call discipleship.

We also know that, regardless of what our contract says, we are youth workers 24/7. The apostle Paul said to the church in Corinth, "Follow my example, as I follow the example of Christ" (1 Corinthians 11:1), and we should be the same. Our lives need to authentically reflect this holy God we proclaim and worship. So it is entirely fair for our young people to expect to be able to watch us and follow our example all the time, not just when we are working. So I would argue that there is no "off duty" for a youth worker.

I would equally argue that there must be places of rest and reflection built in. We need to make space daily to pray and be with God, and take days off in our week to recharge our batteries. The challenge is to come at this from a place of grace, not law. The nature of the role of a youth worker requires working at strange hours. It is a good thing, if working a late night, to try to take some time out elsewhere in that day, or get some rest the day after. However, it isn't always practical or possible, and let's not get legalistic about it (I've known people insist on taking an hour off if they worked an hour extra a day earlier). Work is good, rest is good – I have found the more I worry about keeping the two separate, the more stressed I become; and the less I worry about the separation, the more relaxed and balanced I am.

The bigger question for me in all of this is one of identity. If we find our identity in our role, we will get ourselves into trouble; but if our identity is found in Christ, my experience is that we will manage our boundaries just fine.

Two questions for self-reflection:

• Is my identity based on being a person who follows Christ, or on being a youth worker?

• Am I fulfilling my own emotional needs through my own friends and faith, or through my youth group?

Matt Costley is the youth pastor at Holy Trinity, Brompton. Follow him on twitter @ MattCostley

Further reading

Skills for Collaborative Ministry – Sally Nash, Jo Pimlott, Paul Nash, SPCK, 2011

7

Evaluate and Redefine

So you're off and running. Whether you're starting a new youth-work initiative or rebooting an existing project, you're doing something. All being well, you've got some kind of plan, a team, and a support network to help you achieve it, and even some young people to deliver it for. Now what?

Well, in short, you keep going. Yet, right from the start, you should be finding ways to ask the question: "How is this going"? A commitment to making your youth ministry the best it can be means a constant and endless process of evaluation. Not only that: it also means being prepared to change things that aren't quite working, even if you like them. It means listening to the wise voices around you, including those of the young people you're seeking to serve. This short chapter gives you some simple tools to help you regularly re-evaluate your youth work, and some ideas about how to bring change to a project that's already up and running.

Evaluation toolkit

In the following few pages, you'll find a series of tools that I've designed for your adaptation as you seek to check and evaluate your work. All of them would work well in my local youth-work context, but are unlikely to work perfectly everywhere else. So please don't worry that I'll be offended if you cross out some bits and add others. They are intended to inspire you to take this process of constant re-evaluation and evolution seriously.

The first tool is an *observation* form. This should be given to a well-chosen person who will sit in and observe a youth session for you, and then give some (fairly) objective feedback on what they saw. The second is a simple form that encourages you to check your progress against the vision and aims you set out with. After that you'll find a *problem solver* – a little diagram that helps you to diagnose and address problems as they arise. Finally, you'll find a draft *appraisal form* for you to use with your line manager on an annual basis. That might look like the most boring thing in the world, but it might also be vital if you're in a context in which your leaders struggle to define and understand what you do.

Use these tools only if they're useful; adapt them or create some of your own. The important thing is that you keep on asking that question: "How is this going?" These tools may help you both to ask that question and to begin answering it.

Tool 1: Observation

This is a tool – based on the system used within formal education – that helps you to gain an objective perspective on your youth-work sessions. However, whereas in a school context it is the teacher who is being observed, here the focus is on the youth work itself. If possible, find someone who understands youth work, but isn't part of your team, to sit in on one of your sessions, observe, and fill in the form below. One idea would be to ask another local youth worker – perhaps from a neighbouring church – to do this for you, on the promise that you will reciprocate. This could be a great way to build links with other local youth ministries, and to learn from and serve one another.

When briefing the observer, suggest that they don't approach the form in a linear fashion, but simply make notes in the relevant areas when they notice something worth commenting on. This may mean, for example, that they write nothing in the "health and safety" area, but huge amounts in the "discipline" section. Do not brief them only to comment on the bad things, or the things they would change – you may think you're being humble, but, however secure you are, that observation form will not be helpful when you come to read it back.

Youth-work observation form

Name of observer: _____ Date: _____

Aims of this session (to be completed beforehand by the youth worker):

1. _____

2. _____

3. _____

What did you notice with regard to the following areas?

Entertainment and fun

_____

Group cohesion

_____

Discipline

_____

Input from the session leader

Did you observe any possible health and safety or safeguarding concerns?

_____

What went particularly well?

_____

What did not go so well?

_____

How well did this session achieve the stated aims?

1. _____

2. _____

3. _____

How might this session have been improved?

_____

Tool 2: Aim check

This is simply meant to help you to intentionally return to your stated vision and aims. You could run through the form below on your own, but alternatively you may want to draw your team together to pray and think through your vision and direction. In the first year of a new or rebooted project, you might want to do this every term – after that, once a year is plenty.

In chapter four, I asked you to write a list of two to three dynamic aims for your youth work. Retrieve them now – they make up the first part of the form. If you never got to the point of creating formalized aims and objectives for your youth work, you need to do so before using this tool.

Each question in the form has three answers – this assumes that you have three key aims for your youth work.

Youth-work aim check

The key aims of our youth work (in order of priority) are:

1. _____

2. _____

3. _____

Do your whole team know and understand these aims?

_____

Do your young people know and understand these aims?

_____

Give an example of how each of these aims has been met/furthered in the last term:

1. _____

2. _____

3. _____

Have you done anything that contradicts/undermines these aims?

1. _____

2. _____

3. _____

What could you change in order to better meet these aims?

1. _____

2. _____

3. _____

Tool 3: The problem solver

Youth ministry is never straightforward (and that's the joy of it); inevitably, problems will arise from time to time. Perhaps you're struggling with challenging behaviour, or an activity you're running just isn't capturing anyone's imagination. Often these things can be baffling; under the pressure of trying to lead well, we can struggle to see a clear solution.

This simple diagram is designed to help you think through a problem rather than actually solve it (I'm not a magician!). Each box presents a question – the idea is that you answer each one, and you begin to build up a solution for yourself. You'll be able to answer some questions straight away – others will require you to go and seek help or advice. The idea here is simply to get your thoughts, ideas, and concerns out of your head (where they may be swimming around and causing you stress) and on to paper, and to help you to consider the opinions and input of others. It also encourages you – right at the start – to pray about the problem, which in my experience isn't always the first thing we do when confronted with a challenge.

As with the other tools in this section, you may wish to adapt this diagram for your own context by adding or removing questions. When you fill in the boxes, try to write freely without analysing or editing as you go – no one else needs to see this sheet apart from you, and you may find that by writing in this free-form way you write down something that you hadn't realized before.

As the second box in the diagram makes clear, this isn't suitable for use when faced with a problem that has safety implications – in those cases, seek out your safeguarding officer and/or line manager immediately.

BEFORE YOU START: Pray about the problem – asking God to reveal His wisdom, to bring the right people around you, and to help you find a safe and wise solution.

Describe the problem:

Is there a legal or safeguarding implication in this problem (e.g. is anyone being put at risk of harm)?

IF YES: Contact your appointed safeguarding officer and/or line manager immediately.   **IF NO:** Continue

Who can help you to overcome this problem (either from within your team, or bringing expertise from outside it)?

Talk to your line manager and/or spiritual director about this problem. What is their advice?

How could young people be part of your solution? If appropriate, consult some of them. What is their view?

When realistically could you address this problem? What is a good timescale for seeing it solved?

Who (e.g. parents, young people, rest of team) will you need to communicate with about this problem (and your solution), and when?

What are the first steps you can take to help solve this problem?

Which of your processes and practices need to change in order to allow this problem to be solved/to avoid recurrence of the problem?

Tool 4: Appraisal form

It's good – or rather, essential – practice to have a formal appraisal with your line manager once a year. This applies every bit as much to a lead volunteer as to a full-timer; it is a crucial brick in the wall of accountability, which ensures your youth ministry is safe, well led, and integrated into the wider vision of any church community of which you are part.

Some sections of the form should be completed before the meeting (there are parts for both the appraiser and the person being appraised – appraisee! – to complete in advance), so I would suggest that you complete your sections and then hand the form to your line manager a few days before the meeting, to give them an opportunity to read your comments and add their own.

Block out at least ninety minutes for the meeting itself. The setting should be at least semi-formal – an office rather than a sitting room, for example. I'm not going to be prescriptive about dress code, etc., but the general idea is not to hold the conversation in a relaxed, informal context. This might seem a little strange, but it's actually important in helping both parties to delineate your (hopefully) good, friendly working relationship from any tough questions you may need to address in an appraisal.

Here's the most important thing for you both to remember: this is your appraisal – not your line manager's opportunity for an impromptu disciplinary hearing. You should do about two-thirds of the speaking as a general rule, because this is an opportunity for you to talk about how things are going, any needs you may have, and what you see as your objectives for the coming year.

Once again, feel free to adapt this. You may think this is far too structured or businesslike for your needs, in which case, use it as a template for your own form. You may also prefer to drop the idea of completing part of the form in advance, and make the whole process more collaborative. If you do this, allow at least two hours for the appraisal meeting.

Appraisal Form

Name of appraisee:

_____

Name of appraiser:

_____

Date: Date of last appraisal (if any):

_____

SECTION ONE (To be completed by the appraisee beforehand):

1. What has gone particularly well in the last year? Why did it go well, and what principles/wider lessons could we draw from this?

_____

2. What has not gone so well? What lessons have been learned from this?

_____

3. How have you progressed or achieved your aims/objectives for the last year?

_____

4. How could others help you to better achieve your aims and objectives? Your line manager:

_____

Other colleagues/individuals:

_____

5. Optional: What are your long-term personal goals (professional or otherwise)?

_____

6. How successful is the line-management relationship from your perspective, and how might it be improved?

_____

7. Are there any other issues that haven't been raised earlier?

_____

SECTION TWO (To be completed by the appraiser beforehand):

8. What – from your perspective – do you feel has gone particularly well in the youth work in the past twelve months?

_____

What factors contributed to this success?

_____

9. What hasn't gone so well, or has been more challenging?

_____

What factors have contributed to this?

_____

10. How successful is the line management relationship from your perspective, and how might it be improved?

_____

11. Are there any other issues that haven't been raised earlier?

_____

SECTION THREE (To be completed at the meeting):

12. What are my objectives for the next twelve months? (Choose SMART goals, which are Specific, Measurable, Agreed, Realistic, and Time-bound)

_____

13. What support or resources will I need to complete the above?

_____

14. What training or development needs can you identify together?

_____

Appraisal completed:_____

Appraisee's signature: _____ Date:_____

Appraiser's signature:_____ Date:_____

Redefine

Every youth-work project needs change. No youth ministry is so good that it can always remain static – never having to concern itself with external variables such as culture and the local community. We should always be prepared not only for evolution, but even for revolution – because if the work isn't meeting the needs or objectives that it set out to, standing still means death (not for you, hopefully, but certainly of the project).

That doesn't mean waiting for a project to fail utterly, and then trying to build it up again from scratch (though, hopefully, for some of you, this book will have helped to achieve that); it means embracing change as a permanent and never-ending part of your youth work. It means continually asking the question: what could or should we be doing better, and how?

This short section builds on some of the evaluation tools above, and begins to explore how you go about identifying what needs to change in your youth work, and then how to implement that change.

Identify

The evaluation tools in this chapter will naturally help you to identify problems or potential areas of weakness in your youth work. That appraisal question: "What hasn't gone so well?" is painful, but it's also a vital opportunity for honesty, after which can come improvement. The imperative for ongoing evolution (apologies to creationist readers who keep flinch every time I use that word) is one of the most compelling justifications for all that hard evaluation work I've just made you do. At the same time, don't think that all the answers – and the diagnoses of potential problems – can be found by you and your line manager. There are also other important voices to listen to.

What do the young people say?

This is really important. The participants in (not consumers of!) your youth work may have a better handle on what's not working than you do. Of course, their opinions may be based partly on selfish factors, or they may want to influence you to compromise on one of your core values because they don't yet understand or share it. For instance, if you are working with totally unchurched youth, and their feedback is that they'd rather you dropped your ten-minute "God slot", you need to communicate back to them that this is really important to you and your team. Beyond that caveat, though, you should take their counsel seriously – in my experience, young people are much better than adults at identifying some of the sacred cows that we really could live without. If you don't ask them, though, they may not feel they can tell you, so create a forum for regular feedback.

What does your team say?

Your volunteer team both experience the youth work and understand the rationale behind it. They see where aims, objectives, mission, and vision meet practice. No one is better placed to give you an honest assessment on what does and doesn't work. However, while some volunteers are only too happy to tell you exactly what they think isn't working (bless 'em), others will wait to be asked. So, again, make sure you're creating opportunities for honest feedback, communicating that you do listen to and value such comments.

What does the culture say?

In order to stay relevant to the culture(s) you seek to reach, you need to keep up. If we're not careful, Christian projects can get left behind by the breakneck speed of progression in youth culture(s); we're the ones still running Day-Glo-themed rave nights when everyone else has moved on to hip-hop rap battles. So make an effort to listen to the culture that your young people spend their lives soaking and swimming around in. It's not about trying to be cool and knowing all the words to the latest number one – it's about understanding the stories that young people are consuming and participating in, and the trends that matter to them.

Youthwork magazine is one particularly good (if I do say so myself) resource to help with this; visit www.youthwork.co.uk to learn more.

What does your local context say?

Communities are not static. It may be that your local context has changed markedly since you originally surveyed the opportunities. Take the regeneration of parts of east London for example: before the 2012 Olympic Games, these were areas of social deprivation; now there are million-pound apartments, a mega-mall, and state-of-the-art "legacy" sports facilities. If you had been a youth worker in nearby Stratford over that time, you would have seen the demographics of the local population shift; you might have seen a widening gulf between rich and poor, and issues arising from that; you might have seen a marked change in the needs of local young people. Listen and look out for these kinds of changes in your own community (although they're unlikely to be as drastic); they should inform the way you evolve your youth work.

What does the Lord say?

I'm not going to hammer this one. Much of this book has focused on the need to keep God at the centre of the youth work, and of your own life as leader. Just a tiny reminder, then: don't forget to involve Him when you consider whether things might need to change.

What about when the "tough" kids turn up?
Laura Haddow

It's a familiar feeling. The moment when you look out of the door of your church or youth project to see a bunch of locally-known scary-looking kids coming your way.

As panic momentarily takes hold of you, two choices flash through your mind:

1: Shut the door fast, turn off the lights, and whisper to the well-behaved members of your youth group to put down the Uno cards and remain completely silent.

Or, 2: Take a deep breath, and brace yourself for the chaos.

Even with ten years of youth-work experience behind me, unfortunately I still can't tell you that I have all the answers when it comes to this. The Hub (the youth project I used to run), would often have rival gangs turn up on the doorstep, or young people whose reputation preceded them, and I remember well the fear of not knowing what exactly to do in these situations. When do you close the door quickly? And is that ever the right thing to do?

You need to establish what exactly your aim is with the youth work you are running or thinking of starting. It's hard to do all things well, so think through the needs in your church or location. Who are you trying to reach? Is the need to start a group that will disciple the young people in your church who need support and encouragement in their faith? Or is it to reach out into the local community and contact those who have never heard about Jesus? Be clear in your mind what you are trying to achieve, and that will help in dealing with situations like this. If you decide to have an open-door policy then it's worth thinking through the following:

1: Sit down as a team and agree your limits and rules. It's essential you are all consistent in applying these or they will be no use at times when they are put to the test, as in situations such as this. "Rules" sounds authoritarian, but you need to make sure you have procedures in place to protect the other young people in your care, yourself, and the building.

We had only six simple rules, all of which were easily enforceable. Alongside these rules we operated a three-warning system whereby you would be asked to leave for the night after the third warning. Do you have a banning policy? How long do you ban for? All these things need to be discussed as a team before you open your doors.

2: Pray before and after your youth meetings. Don't get complacent in your youth work; as you prepare, remind yourself that God is at the centre of what you are doing. Pray that, whatever happens during the course of the evening, you will have the wisdom and patience to deal with it in the right way.

3: Remember it's a long-term work. It's a bit of a cliché but so often the kids who have the most behavioural problems are the ones who have lots going on behind the scenes. It's about patience and building trust; they are suspicious of you as much as the other way round. It takes time, but you will get there.

4: Be networked into a good range of agencies in your area – so that when you come upon a problem you will know how to help. It's great to have the aim of seeing all our young people become Christians, but in some cases we need to be able to offer them help and hope with serious issues they face before we begin sharing our faith with them.

5: If possible, befriend your local PCSOs (Police Community Support Officers). You may not think this is necessary in your work, but I've found it a fantastic tool in dealing with difficult young people. They often know a local disruptive young person even better than you do and are happy to pop in from time to time on their rounds. A quick five-minute visit to your youth evening can make all the difference, trust me.

Laura Haddow is an experienced youth worker and is currently Project Development Worker for www.selfharm.co.uk. Follow her on Twitter @laurahaddow

Implement

Having identified what needs to change, you now need to make it happen. This is potentially much trickier than the first half of the equation, because people are much better at verbalizing criticism than they are at practising a better way. With anything other than the smallest change you will face resistance, criticism, and maybe even opposition; your job as a leader is both to listen with integrity and to pursue the right way forward even if not every person agrees (though if a majority don't agree, think very carefully before bulldozing on). The following steps are a rough guide to charting a path through change:

Make change part of the culture

Don't allow the feel of what you do to become stale. If people expect things to evolve, they will be much less concerned when bigger changes occur. If you've met in the same scout hut for forty consecutive Sundays from 8–9.30 p.m., working your way through the book of Leviticus, your group and your team may struggle with a sudden switch to a sport-based drop-in club. If, however, you are often trying new things, enjoy a varied programme, and make it clear that you are always open to feedback and improvement, then change becomes part of the culture of your group – and that naturally makes change easier.

Identify resistance

Try to head problems off in advance if you can. You are likely to know who in your group, your volunteer team, and your church will find change – or a particular change – difficult. Make an effort to talk to these people before you implement change; give them an opportunity to comment on what you are planning, and explain really clearly why it is so important to you. Help them to understand the process of listening and evaluating that has brought you to this point, and try to get to a place of consensus with them. Usually you will find that simply validating these people and their concerns with this kind of honest conversation will be enough to get them on board.

Explain the rationale; take people with you

Don't just change things – explain what you're going to do, and why. There are obviously different levels of change, from switching model completely to doing away with the tuck shop, so you will need to gauge whether this warrants a short announcement or a special meeting. However you choose to do it, make sure you explain why you're changing things, rather than just how. As in the previous point, it's really helpful for people to understand that you have properly evaluated the way things were and listened to God and your young people and more, and sought to involve others in this process all the way along.

Pilot change

This step might not be relevant for the small stuff, but if you're making a big change, you don't need to commit to forever straight away! Try things out. Give a new idea three months, and then evaluate and redefine it if it isn't working. This step will also help the doubters to get behind what you are doing.

Celebrate change

As you do implement, don't sneak change in quietly through the back door. Where relevant, make some noise about the new thing – celebrate the exciting new shape of what you're doing. In doing this, you convey to everyone that you think this new way is better than the old one, and help to create excitement about the future. This probably isn't necessary if you've got rid of the tuck shop, but if you're moving the night you hold your group on, it's vital in helping all the stakeholders to embrace change.

Evaluating and improving what you do isn't just a one-time thing. It is a vital and constant dimension to any successful youth group. Taken seriously, the tools and principles in this chapter can help you to avoid many of the pitfalls that lead to the stagnancy and even death of a youth-work project. It's not a miracle formula – but it's your best shot. Keep questioning what you do and how it could be better; keep listening to others and to God, and remain committed to ongoing change – not for change's sake, but because you are determined that your youth work should continue to serve God and young people as well as it can.

8

FAQs

To close, I asked some of my friends who are either experienced youth workers or in exactly the position this book is aimed to resource, to come up with some honest questions. These are the sorts of problems and concerns that they know from experience will arise when you are initiating or maintaining a youth-work project. I've grouped the questions into rough categories in case you're looking for help with something specific. This chapter exists because it simply wasn't possible to cover every angle of youth ministry in a single book.

I would love to add to this section in future editions of *Youth Work From Scratch*. If you have a question which you think should be included, please email it to martin.saunders@gmail.com

Working for and with a church

Q: How do you integrate young people into church?

A: This is a million-dollar question, and the answer depends hugely on the kind of youth group you run, and the kind of church that you're hoping to integrate your young people into. Youth workers have struggled with this question particularly since youth ministry has begun to drift towards a more relational model, whereas church services themselves tend to be very focused on the programme.

Two basic principles, though, may help. First, integrating young people into church doesn't necessarily mean bringing them into the church service. Although it's desirable that they experience and become comfortable with worship services now (because that's going to make it a lot easier for them to stick around in the long term), it's more vital that they become part of the church family. So are they prayed for by members of the adult congregation – and do they get the opportunity to do the reverse? Are they welcomed and provided for at events your church might run (do your gender-specific "ministry" meetings, e.g. men's breakfast, have a lower age limit – either enforced or implied)? Do they ever get mentioned on noticeboards or in newsletters? The welcome your church extends to young people must extend beyond the youth group itself if you want them to feel part of things.

Second, you should think about participation. If you want young people to take part in your services, then you have to allow them opportunities to be part of those services! That doesn't just mean inviting young people to be on the music rota – although that's a start – but also taking the risk of having them on the welcoming team, leading prayers, and even – Lord have mercy – preaching. When I tag-team preached a sermon with a seventeen-year-old lad in my group recently, it was the best feedback I'd ever received... and I don't think that was down to my contribution. Giving young people opportunities to serve and participate in church is scary – for you, your leadership, and sometimes the congregation – but it can have two fantastic outcomes: young people feel genuinely part of the church, and the rest of the congregation have their preconceptions challenged, and often hear God speak through the young people.

Q: What do you do when
your vision for youth work
doesn't marry up with that
of the church leadership?

A: Pray. That's the first place to start, and so many of us – myself the worst of sinners – articulate questions like this before getting on our knees before God over the problem. Once you've done that, however, if things don't change, you have to hold two things in tension: the authority of your leaders, and the vision that you believe God has given you – and the reality is that this is difficult.

The first and most important principle in trying to walk this road is maintaining your own integrity. I understand the pain of trying to do youth work under a church leadership that doesn't "get it", but I have no time for those who see this as a licence to moan, criticize, and gossip about that leadership, not only to their volunteer team, but also to their young people. What on earth does that communicate to them? So guard your heart and your tongue as you walk this road.

Moving on from that, however, there is nothing wrong with your appropriately challenging the leadership on this. As you make your case, try to start from their perspective. If they are concerned that you want to do too much "detached" work, they probably hold concerns that the Christian young people will be neglected. So what about building a vision that involves those Christian teenagers in the detached work? Or, for example, if they want you to hold a termly "youth service", and you don't like the idea, what about turning the tables and inviting the whole church to one of your youth sessions? This may satisfy their concern that young people are visibly integrating with the rest of the congregation, but you're able to do so on terms that the young people will be happy with. Plus, it would be great to watch some of the elderly folk playing dodgeball…

Ultimately, though, this point of tension has been the reason why many youth workers have given up, handed on the baton, or left their church. If there's a problem, it's best to recognize it early, and to keep conversation about it live and healthy with your line manager. Sometimes the solution is a very gradual process of vision alignment, which takes place only after you and your leadership have learned to love and trust each other. Sometimes it can feel as if this process moves about as quickly as an elderly tortoise, but it's worth it in the end.

Young people

Q: How should you react when one of your teenagers tells you she's pregnant – and what does this mean for the group going forward?

A: We all make mistakes. It's just that some of them are more physically obvious than others. This must be the message that we communicate to all our young people when this happens – unplanned teenage pregnancy is regrettable, but in God's economy a mistake is a mistake like any other, and, through Jesus, just as forgivable.

The issue really isn't about your reaction (which I hope will be caring, concerned, and most of all full of love, not judgment), but what you do next. I've seen a young person basically abandoned by her youth worker at this point, because that person's ego had been so badly bruised by the fact that one of "their" young people had done this. It isn't about you at all – but the terrifying prospect of what lies ahead for this girl is a fantastic opportunity for you to help, love, and even disciple her. This is a job for a female youth worker, so if you're not one, find a volunteer you really trust to take your place (or if you're married, see if your wife is able to help). Assuming it's you, though, you should now offer to be as involved in the next nine months as the girl wants – which may involve accompanying her to appointments, or simply being around regularly to talk things through.

Now, and when the baby comes along, you – the lead youth worker – must become this girl's biggest advocate, to the group and to the rest of the church. Challenge gossip or "tutting" when you come across it; take every opportunity to publicly affirm, encourage, and normalize her (although not to the point of embarrassing her). When the baby arrives, work hard to make sure she can still take part in the group – even if that means holding meetings at her house or finding a babysitter so she can come to church. And if, as many girls today do, she decides that abortion is the only route for her, avoid being judgmental and try to offer whatever support she may need – there are various Christian agencies working in this area.

What you do in reaction to this news could be definitive for the rest of this young person's life and faith. So react with love!

How do you get young people to adopt justice as a lifestyle?

Matt Valler

Jesus challenged the stereotypes of his day, stood with the poorest, and embraced the marginalized. His way was practical, and as disciples and disciple-makers our following of Jesus needs to be practical too. Justice isn't a theme on a list to tick off. It's something to live for. God is on a mission to redeem and remake the world and calls us to join Him. So doing the "justice activity" here and the "justice moment" there isn't enough to really make God's story part of our own.

But how do we actually make justice part of everyday life, and how do we bring that into our youth work? Because the reality is that as leaders we often feel pretty overwhelmed by the scale of poverty and injustice in the world. Our heroes – people like Martin Luther King, or Mother Teresa, or Gandhi – just seem so exceptional. And exceptional feels beyond me. But ordinary I can do!

Ordinary is all that is needed. Living a different way by following Jesus is for ordinary people who want to take a step and place their foot in His footprint. Each step brings movement, and together those steps begin to form rhythms, patterns of everyday life that change the way we live.

Making moments

So let's get practical. Justice moments can never be the whole story in our youth work but they can have the important effect of grabbing attention and providing a challenge, which can really galvanize energy. Experiential challenges are very effective. Try Slum Survivor, from Soul Action, or The No Slumber Challenge, from Tearfund. Or organize a sponsored twenty-four-hour fast and, if you can, gather together for all or part of the time.

Other challenges can run throughout a week alongside normal life. For example, as a group you could agree that you will all sleep on the floor for a few nights in solidarity with the 150 million children who sleep rough each night. You could get sponsored to do this – but that doesn't have to be the main focus. There is something very powerful about making ourselves uncomfortable in order to let the reality of the world get to our body rather than just our mind. It doesn't make any immediate difference to street children, but it can be a very significant part of character formation, which generally has far more impact in the long term than a one-off event.

Other ideas like this are The Water Challenge and The Rice & Beans Challenge, both from Tearfund, or Live Below the Line, from the Global Poverty Project.

Building rhythms

These big challenges can become pretty overwhelming, so helping young people to take small actions can be very empowering. For example, making a choice to buy fairly traded chocolate this week, adding their name to an online petition, and posting a stat about global poverty as a Facebook status are all really achievable things for a young person. But together they begin to form a rhythm of speaking out on behalf of people in poverty. If we can help young people build that kind of rhythm, then justice starts to embed itself in day-to-day life. That's how we can move beyond the justice "moment" and let God's story make its way into our everyday.

Another example would be to encourage actions such as forfeiting a coffee or a snack and text-donating the equivalent amount, contributing to a weekly group collection in support of a justice charity, or deciding to hold the door open for someone else every time you walk through one. All these are achievable things that together begin to form a rhythm of generosity.

This generation of young people are more interested in doing than in observing, more interested in real experiences than in abstract discussions. Not only can we help young people engage with justice in their everyday life, but doing so can be one of the best ways to engage young people per se – both churched and unchurched. It's in making justice a discipleship lifestyle that faith becomes alive and Jesus really begins to make sense.

Matt Valler is Project Leader at Bible Engagement for Youth International Coalition. He previously led the Rhythms project, which aims to inspire a generation to live differently. For an extensive practical toolkit for helping young people build rhythms to change their world, visit www.rhythms.org

Volunteers

Q: What do you do with a
bad volunteer that you've
"inherited"?

A: In chapter three we looked in detail at how to build a team of volunteers, but when you inherit a team things can be more complicated. If you're coming into a situation where youth work has already been running, there may already be a volunteer team in place who feel ownership of the work. They may feel excited by and enthusiastic about your appearance on the scene, or alternatively they may feel threatened. It's vital that you meet individually with each of your volunteers – even if only for a short time – and in the course of that conversation you will hopefully be able to build the beginning of a good working relationship, and establish some common ground. If you're intuitive, you may be able to work out from this initial encounter whether one of your volunteers might be a "bad fit", but this might not come to your attention until much later.

Obviously this question uses the word "bad" as shorthand. If you realize that one of your volunteers is behaving or speaking inappropriately, being generally unreliable or struggling to influence the young people positively, I would suggest you treat this person as you would someone you had personally invited to join the team – rather than as a problem to get rid of. Meet with them informally to raise the issue; try to offer advice, help, and support, and only then – if this doesn't work – elevate to a more formal meeting and then possibly ask them to step down, if necessary.

If their actions put a young person at risk in any way, however, you will act more formally – and quickly. Inform your line manager (and, if appropriate, your safeguarding officer) about the problem, and make sure that your communication with parents (if needed) is clear and open.

In general, however, try to avoid writing off and clearing the decks of volunteers you have inherited. They were holding the fort faithfully before you came along, and the young people probably love them. Try to find a role that suits them in your new-look team – you may discover that your "bad" volunteer was actually just working with the wrong age group or doing the wrong job.

Q: How do you get a balance between recruiting much-needed volunteers and being smart about choosing potential role models?

A: The reality is that, in many places, you will not have the luxury of a huge field of candidates all desperate to serve in the youth ministry. Even in my own church, which has well over 500 regular members, we struggle to recruit the numbers of volunteers we need – this problem has only been more exaggerated in the smaller churches I've served in. This obviously doesn't mean that you should get people involved in the youth work who are totally unsuited to it, but it does mean that you may need to work with some "rough diamonds", to find a role that might be a good fit for them. Not everyone needs to be an up-the-front leader, or take the lead in small-group discussion. The people who may not relish or be suited to that kind of job may be only too thrilled to lead games, run the tuck shop, make sure everyone is out of your building on time, or set up the venue at the start. They might be incredibly quiet around young people, but also brilliant at observing and listening to them.

But this doesn't address the question of role models – and here we have to ask: what does make a good role model? In youth ministry, it is someone who helps to model to young people what it means to follow Christ as an adult. So, if their behaviour demonstrates the opposite of that, it's probably counter-productive to have them on your youth team. But don't be a Pharisee – we all make mistakes, and we all have problems that we're still dealing with. I am not suggesting you discount anyone who has ever made a mistake; rather that those who choose to go on making those mistakes publicly are not good volunteer candidates. So, for me, a single mum who has never been married could make a great volunteer and could be a fantastic role model; a young man who frequently displays his wealth by way of flashy jewellery, sports car, and tales of expensive hi jinks, probably wouldn't be either.

Q: How do you resolve and defuse tension between two members of your volunteer team?

A: Volunteers can sometimes seem superhuman – but from time to time we realize that they're not. Like everyone else, they can fall into conflict with other people, and unfortunately sometimes those people are also on our volunteer team.

If this happens to you, don't let it fester – the conflict could quickly escalate, divide your team, and, worst of all, spread to your young people (who will be hugely affected by this behaviour, and not in a good way). So, as soon as you've established some facts, get everyone involved into a room together (unless the situation makes this wildly inappropriate – in which case, meet them individually). Pray with each person, and then talk the situation through. Apply conch-shell rules – each person gets to put their side across uninterrupted, with you acting as mediator. Although the resolution may be for one of these people to step down from your team, applying these principles of early intervention, prayer, and listening gives you your best chance of a good outcome. This will also model healthy conflict resolution to any other leaders or young people who have become aware of the problem.

Group dynamics

Q: What if you have only a handful of young people?

A: I hope that the answer to this is contained in the first part of the book – that you develop your ministry around those young people and their needs. Trouble is, we can get very fixated on numbers – especially when they're either very low or very high – and, as hard as this is, numbers mustn't take too much of your focus. Of course we want to see as many young people as possible reached with the transformational love of God, but not at the expense of those He has already entrusted to us. So – develop your ministry first around those young people and their needs – and then look outwards.

How do you look outwards? Fortunately, you already have a potent group of evangelists at your disposal – that small group of young people. They all have friends, and those friends all have interests – so talk to your young people about the kinds of events and activities that you could put on, and which would attract their friends. This sounds like the most simple advice in the world, but how often do we follow it? Help your young people to reach their friends, and you may see your group grow very naturally.

Q: How do you incorporate a young person with additional physical or learning needs into your youth group?

A: This is a hugely important area, and one which requires a greater brain than mine. The box from Ian Macdonald (see next page) gives more practical advice from experience, and organizations such as Children Worldwide (www.childrenworldwide.co.uk) are on hand to help resource this area.

A couple of points of common sense, however: you may want to ask a specific volunteer leader to keep an eye on this young person and their needs, but I would suggest that, if possible, you don't make this a formal thing (so they don't always need to sit together). This avoids unnecessarily stigmatizing the young person, or communicating that they need a "carer" at all times, when perhaps they don't.

It's absolutely vital that you develop a good relationship with the young person's parent(s), and establish clear lines of communication. Depending on the nature of the additional need, the parent(s) will be quite anxious about how their child will get on, enjoy themselves, and integrate with the rest of the group, so try to put yourself in their position and communicate as much as you can (including plenty of positives) about how this is going. That good relationship is also important because sometimes you may need to contact them during an activity for advice, or even to ask them to collect their child if things have all got too much.

I should underline how important it is that we try to get this area right. God is for all people, as is His church – and we need to think seriously about the accessibility of our youth ministry. If you find this a bit overwhelming (in the sense that you don't feel that you'd do a very good job of looking after young people with additional needs), then there may be people within your congregation or community who have expertise that they'd be willing to share. Feeling nervous about getting this area "wrong" is understandable and fine – just don't let it become a barrier to your extending the offer of Jesus to all young people in your area.

Inclusivity from scratch
Ian Macdonald

Writing something generic about inclusion, given the range of additional or special needs that there are, is quite a challenge. However, coming from the perspective of a youth worker who has faced the challenge of inclusion, and my own experiences of having a son who has cerebral palsy, I wanted to try to frame some advice and thinking.

Being inclusive is a great way of modelling (and experiencing) the kingdom of God. Young people with additional needs can be a great blessing to the group as well as being blessed by the group.

Don't worry about what you don't know! Talk to the individual young person first and foremost; get to know them. If speech is a difficulty for them, don't be frightened; listen – really listen, and admit it if you are struggling to understand. See the young person, not the disability. If you want to know more, talk to the parent(s); they'll be more than happy to help you understand the young person's needs and challenges. But come to this conversation having got to know the young person a little. Remember you are good at relating to young people; don't become something different because they have a disability. If they have a diagnosed condition, a bit of reading and preparation time on the internet can also be really helpful.

Having worked with the parent(s) to understand the needs, make sure you work with the young person in the context of the group. Parents can have a limited view of what their son/daughter can do and wants to do (all parents rightly want to protect their children, but parents of children with disabilities can sometimes develop quite concerned and restrictive views of what they are capable of). The group may be a great opportunity for them to explore more of who they are and what they are able to do. Listen – really listen.

Inclusion will require additional thought, planning, and/or people depending on the young person. On a very practical level some young people may not fit into neat age divisions and you may want to include them at "stage" not age. Work to make activities work for all of the group. Review regularly with the young person and the parents.

And, finally, as a parent can I just say what a blessing it is to see your child loved, valued, and included regardless of their ability.

In summary:

1. There is much to be gained as a group (and for you as a leader) in being inclusive.

2. Work with the parents to understand the young person and their challenges/needs.

3. Having gleaned understanding from the parents, seek to get to know the young person. (Their view of what they need and who they are may differ from their parents' view).

4. Remember to take account of the needs of ALL your young people in planning.

Ian Macdonald is the Diocesan Youth Adviser for Oxford, and the founder of brilliant long-running youth ministry website, Youthblog, www.youthblog.org

Money

Q: What ideas do you have for youth work on a shoestring budget?

A: If money is tight, then the best advice is to start small. It could be that you have set up a youth-work initiative with little or no budget, and very quickly this can become frustrating if your plans outgrow your financial capabilities. Be realistic about what you can achieve without much money – and, unless you're particularly wealthy, don't start subsidizing the work from your own pocket. That might sound anti-generous, but the problem is that it might not be sustainable; if your group grows, so might your costs; you could be left in a situation where you personally can't afford for the work to get any bigger! Instead – and if your church budget really is too stretched to help – look at alternative sources of income. A few practical ideas:

- Consider charging a small fee for some activities. If you're holding an open youth club, for instance (which may have overheads), young people will not be put off by, say, a £1 entry charge. If you struggle with that concept, simply make the charge a voluntary donation, but make it clear that there are costs involved in running the project.

- Take an offering as part of your worship. This has the key benefit of teaching your young people to be generous and to see giving as a spiritual discipline. It also has the additional benefit of bringing in some much-needed cash to help fund your activities!

- Explore whether you could be eligible for any grant income (see next question).

- Ask your young people to help you raise money for the group (see next question).

Aside from bringing more money in, you can still structure a great programme of activities with low or zero costs. Going on a countryside ramble (night or day) is free; getting together to discuss the Bible costs nothing; outdoor sports need minimal equipment and a public park. Even if you've got a massive youth budget, it's actually good practice to celebrate the free things in life – doing so communicates something powerful to young people in a consumerist age, and prevents your group from being another thing that they "consume".

Q: How do you get started with fund-raising?

A: There may be some expertise within your church leadership or community on this front. If your church is old it will certainly have raised funds for repairs; if there are accountants, fund-raisers, or financial specialists within your congregation, then you have access to people who understand how the financial side of all this works. Find these people if they exist in your context, and make them lots of tea and biscuits while asking politely for their help.

The best youth fund-raising campaigns are initiated by – and as far as possible run by – young people. This not only accesses their God-given creativity; it also gives them an opportunity for ownership and participation. So, if you're looking to raise some money for an overseas trip, a new minibus, or simply some new resources, get your young people together and ask them for their ideas. I've seen some brilliant examples of this recently in my own youth group, where young people have shown the ingenuity to raise large and small sums, but the key factor has always been this: in every case they've grasped a vision. Whether that's the group of girls who raised nearly £10,000 to fight human trafficking, or the sixteen-year-old who decided to give a percentage of her babysitting income to the church building fund – each of them caught hold of a clear vision, and saw how their actions could have an impact on it.

Beyond this, you may find that your youth work is eligible for grant income from a charitable trust or even a local government budget. Do some research locally to see if this is likely – find out who is responsible for youth work at your local council, and ask them about this; ask your church leadership to help you to find out whether there are any local trusts that have an interest in youth work. I know of Christian projects that receive literally hundreds of thousands of pounds from these sources each year. A note of caution, though: while you shouldn't hide the faith element of what you do, it will be a barrier for some funders. If with integrity you can request funds for a part of your work that is not specifically faith-focused, such as an open youth club, you may find you have more success with funders who stipulate that they do not finance the promotion of a faith.

Other adults

Q: How do you partner with parents?

A: Parents are your key allies. For every hour that young people spend in your care, they spend ten or twenty under their parents' roof. Whether they like it or not, they are hugely influenced by their parents' world views and opinions, so, regardless of whether they personally have a faith, these men and women will have an impact on whether a young person feels positively or negatively towards your group or church. In the first instance, then, you should work to help all parents understand that you and your group are positive influences in the lives of their sons and daughters. Hold gatherings for parents at least twice a year – a barbecue in the summer, and Christmas drinks and nibbles, for instance. Use the time to explain (appropriately) some of your vision for the youth group, to tell some stories about the good things that have happened recently, and most importantly to build up your relationship with them. There may be some members of your volunteer team who are particularly good at the latter, so make sure you employ them well on the day!

Beyond this, however, there is a vital role that Christian parents play, and that's in the faith development of their children. Christian parents will take this aspect of child-raising seriously, but in most cases will also feel out of their depth and presume that they're doing a bad job. So part of your role in "partnering" with them isn't just about getting them to help you, but also about being available to advise and encourage them in their "faith parenting". You shouldn't do this without an invitation, but in my experience many parents are hoping that their youth worker will be able to give some advice about how to incorporate faith into the family's home life. When their children were small this seemed easy enough: grace at dinner and prayers before bed. When their children grow older, many parents are nonplussed about how to continue practising faith as a family.

You may even want to hold a very different kind of gathering for parents, then, perhaps with an external speaker who has experience of raising teenagers (this may or may not have a faith dynamic). Parenting classes tend to cater for parents of under-fives – yet that's not when the process of bringing up children ends! It could be that the parents of your group members are desperate for some advice in this area, and you could be the one to connect them with it.

Q: How do you deal with unhappy local residents who complain about the noise levels of, say, the Friday night drop-in and who threaten to go to the authorities?

A: This is a really tough one, because these people possibly feel they have no stake in or responsibility for the lives of the young people in your care. You could try to hold a meeting for local residents, at which you listen to their concerns, explain your plan for improving the situation, and also point out that by giving local teenagers a safe place to congregate, you are potentially diverting them from hanging out on the street – something which most local residents dislike even more than noise!

Realistically, though, this approach may be problematic; you may struggle to get these people along to a meeting, and you may not feel equipped to face them in this context. The more practical answer, then, is that, while establishing a clear line of communication with these residents – probably through simple letters or emails – you should try to address the issue of noise. Could moving some events to a different part of your venue help to reduce sound levels? Can you establish some simple rules about not congregating outside the venue? In my experience, young people often feel like demonized members of their local community anyway, so I wouldn't advocate telling them that complaints have been made. Rather, approach the issue from the proactive angle of wanting to be respectful to your neighbours.

Going away

Q: What are "residentials",
and how do I get started?

A: A "residential" weekend is an opportunity to take your youth group away. You may choose to book your group into a purpose-built activity centre (see http://www.cci.org.uk for all the help you could possibly need), or, alternatively, find a safe, appropriate venue yourself.

The strength of this sort of weekend is its intensity. Your young people live, eat, do chores, have fun, pray, worship, and learn about God together non-stop for forty-eight hours; doing this will profoundly bond and strengthen the group. Many youth workers report that more is achieved – with regard to both group dynamics and faith development – over the space of two days away than in an entire term of weekly youth meetings.

Try to plan the event far enough in advance so that everyone can get it into their diaries, any concerns from parents can be assuaged, and, crucially – you have enough time to plan something really memorable. Make sure you have enough leaders (you might be able to persuade some nice people from your church to come along and be your chefs!), and establish safe rules for the getaway including minibus/travel behaviour, and single-sex dorms/bedrooms! In your planning, consider three important things:

- Make sure it's safe. Do thorough risk assessments, and make sure you pay a visit to the venue in advance.

- Get creative. This is your chance to really have fun and unleash the creativity of your team! Plan surprises. I know of one youth worker who organized artificial snow in the middle of the night, then woke all his youth up at 3 a.m. to enjoy it! You might not have his budget or contacts, but that's no reason not to think creatively and make your getaway memorable.

- Make proper time for God. Getting away from home for forty-eight hours is a fantastic opportunity for young people to leave their usual stresses behind and engage fully with God. Develop a programme for the weekend that is packed with fun, but also gives significant time to exploring a theme or section of the Bible. Over the space of several sessions – perhaps Friday night, Saturday morning, Saturday night, and Sunday morning – you can really take your group on a journey that could prove transformational.

Q: What are the advantages of taking young people to summer camps and festivals?

A: Camps and festivals offer young people the opportunity of a "mountain-top" faith experience. They are surrounded with hundreds, thousands or even tens of thousands of other young Christians (or at least young people who are open to faith); they spend several days effectively receiving a very hip and fun form of religious instruction! By the end of such an event, young people have heard powerful stories, enjoyed engaging in worship, had the Bible explained to them relevantly, and all along have done so in the context of having fun with their friends. Of course they return on a high!

However, the big problem with "mountain-top" experiences is that they are inevitably followed by a trip down into the "valley"! Emotional reactions do not last for ever, and within a few months some young people will even be questioning whether what they had perceived as "meeting with God" was simply the result of hype and hysteria. Youth leaders must be mindful of this, and encourage a more sustainable reaction. Two things may help: firstly, consider developing a programme for the term after the camp (probably the autumn term) that picks up on some of the themes that were addressed there, and also seeks to replicate some of the practical aspects. So, if you went to a festival with sung worship and prayer ministry, why not spend a term doing these things in your youth-group meetings? Secondly, consider exploring the ancient spiritual disciplines with young people – before, during, and after the event. These practical tools help young people to own and develop a deeper faith – you'll find a full curriculum for this in my book *The Beautiful Disciplines*.

Camps, like residentials, are so impactful because of their intensity. In the space of four or five days, you'll see young people (and their faith) radically alter before your eyes. Sometimes this change is naturally permanent; more often, it requires help from you – the local youth leader – to ensure that it is more than simply a short-term "high".

Safeguarding

Q: Is it ever appropriate for a leader to be alone with a young person (i.e. when giving them a lift home)?

A: Sometimes this is going to be necessitated by circumstance (e.g. a young person is stranded at your venue and needs a lift home), and it is not actually illegal, but the word "appropriate" is the crucial one here. Wherever possible, take steps to avoid being left alone with a young person – especially one of the opposite sex. In a mentoring context, this doesn't mean you can't meet one to one – just make sure you don't meet in a closed room with no one else nearby. I tend to meet young people for coffee, rather than at church or home; some youth workers I know meet in a room with lots of windows, in view of church colleagues on the other side.

If you really do have cause to be alone with a young person, try to communicate this need to their parents, and another leader or responsible adult, BEFOREHAND. This at least ensures that everyone is clear that you have not engineered the situation, and are only in it as a last resort.

Q: How many youth leaders are the minimum for any group?

A: Strictly speaking, there is no minimum number stipulated by law. However, common sense and good youth-work practice sometimes require us to go beyond what the law expects. As an absolute sensible minimum, then, any group you run (including small groups) should have at least two adults present; running a group with just one exposes both the adult and the young people to an unnecessary element of risk. In addition, mixed sex groups should always have leaders of both sexes – and to complicate things further it is again advisable to have at least two of each. If a young person were to make a disclosure of abuse to an adult leader, for instance, having two leaders of the same sex on site may make the process that follows much more comfortable for the young person involved. Ideally, then, you will have at least four adult leaders – two male, two female – although of course in many situations this simply won't be possible at first. It's a good aim to work towards, though.

If you run small/cell groups with adult leaders (as we do at my church), this idea might sound a bit worrying – especially if your team is already stretched. However, I have always used this as a great opportunity to partner with parents. If you're meeting in one of the young people's homes, ask if one of their parents is prepared to be in the house – and visible – during your meetings. This satisfies the need for a second adult to be present without the need for yet another leader recruitment drive, and as a handy side effect helps you to find a key ally among your teens.

Afterword

And that's it. I hope that, within these pages, you've found enough inspiration and resources to get you up and running (or back up and running). No one said it would be easy, but what I can promise you is that, to those of us who understand, youth ministry is the highest, most exhilarating, and ultimately rewarding calling imaginable. I pray that this resource will help you to pursue, practise, and enjoy that calling.

So may you see miracles of transformation among the young people with whom you work.

May you catch glimpses of God at work in your community, and in the lives of the teenagers He loves so much.

May you run great youth work that operates with integrity, safety, and passion.

And may you have an absolute blast along the way!

Also from Monarch Books:

The Ideas Factory
Martin Saunders

100 ADAPTABLE DISCUSSION STARTERS TO GET TEENS
TALKING

ISBN: 978-1-85424-834-3   £12.99 UK
ISBN: 978-0-8254- 6173-6 $14.99 US

The Ideas Factory is a priceless PHOTOCOPIABLE resource for
youth leaders.

The 100 spreads contain a story on the left-hand page,
matched by questions on the right. Each explores a topic
pertinent to young people, such as drugs, truancy, or parental
relationships; or an important biblical concept, such as giving,
the afterlife, or love. The questions begin with general issues,
before moving on to what the Bible has to say.

The last 25 discussion starters provide a journey through the main stories and themes
of the Bible.

The Think Tank
Martin Saunders

100 ADAPTABLE DISCUSSION STARTERS TO GET
TEENS TALKING

ISBN: 978-1-85424-964-7   £12.99 UK / $15.99 US

This book contains 100 FREE TO PHOTOCOPY stories designed
to provoke discussion, followed by penetrating questions which
relate the stories to biblical bedrock.

The stories are in four parts:

● **WOULD YOU BELIEVE IT?** – Unbelievable stories,
  all absolutely true!

● **INSPIRING INDIVIDUALS** – Stories of celebrities, public figures and other people of note
  making a positive difference.

● **WHAT WOULD YOU DO?** – Ethics explored through stories, many based on real events.

● **TALKING MOVIES** – A major bonus: 25 movie clips that pack a punch with young people,
  and all the background and questions you'll need to facilitate discussion around them.

www.lionhudson.com

The Beautiful Disciplines
Martin Saunders

HELPING YOUNG PEOPLE DEVELOP THEIR SPIRITUAL ROOTS

ISBN: 978-0-85721-055-5   £12.99 UK / $16.99 US

Packed with practical activities, engaging stories, and relevant explanations, this photocopiable resource will be a powerful tool to help young people develop a deep-rooted and lasting faith.

Martin believes that many young believers today practise a dangerously brittle faith. They need to be led deeper, to a faith sustained not by the personalities of their leaders or by the hype of big events, but by a disciplined direct relationship with God.

This book will help youth leaders to teach their teenagers to pray, study the Bible, live more simply, and discover the value in other ancient disciplines such as fasting, solitude, study and worship.

There are 10 short chapters, one for each session. Each begins with background information for the leader, then provides a photocopiable study section with practical exercises. Each includes questions suitable for discussion in small groups.

"Inclusive, warm, fun and full of passion. Yet the contents are dynamite. Putting the truths and principles of this book into practice will revolutionise your life."

– Mike Pilavachi, in his foreword

"A practical, accessible curriculum that trusts young people's capacity to encounter God. Martin understands the creative power of the ancient disciplines to open the lives of young people to the beauty and freedom of Christian life."

– Mark Yaconelli, author of **Contemplative Youth Ministry**

www.lionhudson.com

500 Prayers for Young People
Martin Saunders

PRAYERS FOR A NEW GENERATION

ISBN: 978-0-85721-017-3   £9.99 UK / $14.99 US

Here are 500 prayers for every occasion. Prayers for relationships; for problems; for saying thank you; for crying out in anger or pain; for times of spiritual dryness; for times of starting again. They can be used for worship together, and for worship alone. They can open up new possibilities, and help to bring a bad day to a better close.

"The desire and need to pray is created inside each one of us at the same time we get spleens, eyeballs and collarbones," says Martin Saunders. "There's nothing special about most of these prayers. But the act of prayer can be very special indeed, and sends humble little people like you and me into the gravitational pull of the almighty God. Prayer is one of the most powerful resources in the universe."

This book is primarily for use by young people themselves, but it will also prove a valuable resource for worship leaders and youth workers. It will make an excellent baptism or confirmation gift from a parent, grandparent or godparent.

www.lionhudson.com